The False Dichotomy of Capitalism and Socialism

A Christian Alternative

Written by Virgil A. Walker

Published by House Walker Publishing

HOUSE WALKER
PUBLISHING

The False Dichotomy of Capitalism and Socialism: A Christian Alternative

The False Dichotomy of Capitalism and Socialism: A Christian Alternative

Introduction 11

Chapter 1: The False Dichotomy 14

Section: 1. The Cage-Fight That Ate the Century 14

Section: 2. "Private vs. State": The Question That Was Never the Real Question 16

Section: 3. How the Dichotomy Was Forged 17

Section: 4. The Secret Agreement Beneath the Noise 19

Section: 5. The Human Cost of the Truce 21

Section: 6. The Door They Bricked Up 25

Section: 7. Breaking Out of the Cage 26

Chapter 2: The Human Scale 28

Section:1. The Creature Who Needs a Garden 28

Section: 2. Aristotle's Forgotten Sentence 29

Section: 3. Thomas Aquinas and the Family as the First Economy 31

Section: 4. Martin Luther and the Household Economy (Oeconomia) 34

Section: 5. The Sabbath Pattern Written Into Creation 35

Section: 6. "Neither Mine Nor Thine, But Ours": Acts 2 and 4 Read Correctly 38

Section: 7. The Parable of the Talents as Distributist Manifesto 41

Section: 8. The Medieval Synthesis in One Paragraph 44

Section: 9. The Scale God Became 46

Chapter 3: Chesterton and Belloc 49

Section: 1. Why We Are Reading Them Slowly 49

Section: 2. The Nine Best Pages of The Outline of Sanity (1926) 53

Section: 3. The Ten Best Pages of The Servile State (1912) 56

Section: 4. Where They Agreed, Where They Differed, Why It Doesn't Matter 58

Section: 5. The Prophecies That Came True (and the One That Hasn't Yet) 61

Section: 6. A Personal Note from the Author to the Reader .. 64

Chapter 4: A Short History of the Road Not Taken 66

Section: 1. The Map We Were Never Shown 66

Section: 2. The Long Memory: Medieval England, Flanders, and Tuscany (1100–1500) 67

Section: 3. The Catholic Countryside That Refused to Die..... 71

Section: 4. The 19th-Century Fight-Back 73

Section: 5. The 20th-Century Miracles 76

Section: 6. The American Experiments Nobody Talks About 79

Section: 7. The Places That Are Doing It Right Now 81

Section: 8. The Pattern That Always Wins 84

Chapter 5: Capitalism's Children 86

Section: 1. The Promise and the Bait-and-Switch 86

Section: 2. The Vanishing Middle: Wealth Concentration in Real Time 88

Section: 3. The Family Under the Algorithm 90

Section: 4. The New Digital Feudalism 93

Section: 5. The Spiritual Wound 96

Section: 6. The Myth of the Meritocracy 99

Section: 7. The Verdict from Inside the Machine 101

Chapter 6: Socialism's Children 104

Section: 1. The Promise This Time 104

Section: 2. The Historical Scorecard 106

Section: 3. The Family in the Collective 109

Section: 4. The New Socialist Serfdom 111

Section: 5. The Spiritual Wound, Part II 114

Section: 6. The Convergence 117

Section: 7. The Quiet Confession of the Survivors 120

Chapter 7: The Distributist Difference 123

Section: 1. The One Thing Both Systems Got Wrong 123

Section: 2. The Core Principle in One Sentence 125

Section: 3. The Tools That Already Exist 127

Section: 4. Red Toryism: A Modern Echo in Conservative Thought 129

Section: 5. Seven Living Proofs You Can Visit Today 131

Section: 6. The Family That Ownership Saves 134

Section: 7. Answering the "Yeah, But…" Chorus 137

Section: 8. The Beauty That Only Ownership Unlocks 140

Section: 9. Starting Where You Stand 142

Chapter 8: Beauty, Sabbath, and the Leisure of Ownership 145

Section: 1. The Forgotten Hunger 145

Section: 2. Leisure Is Not Idleness 147

Section: 3. The Return of the Sabbath Economy 149

Section: 4. Craftsmanship as Prayer 152

Section: 5. The Festival That Cannot Be Bought 154

Section: 6. A Civilization Worth Inheriting 156

Chapter 9: Answering the Objectors 159

Objection: 1. "It's Utopian – Human Nature Is Too Selfish" 159

Objection: 2. "It's Nostalgic – We Can't Go Back to Three Acres and a Cow" 161

Objection: 3. "It Can't Scale in a Global Economy" 163

Objection: 4. "It Will Stifle Innovation" 165

Objection: 5. "It's Anti-Technology / Anti-Progress" 168

Objection: 6. "It's Just Catholicism in Disguise" 170

Objection: 7. "The State/Corporations Will Never Allow It" 172

Objection: 8. "It's Too Slow – We Need Solutions Now" 175

Objection: 9. "Nice in Theory, But Nobody Actually Wants It" 177

Objection: 10. "Yes, But… (The Final Parries)" 179

Objection: 11 "But Who Pays for the Roads? (And Who Pays for Anything Else?)" 181

Objection: 12. "No Political Parties Push for This Economic Plan" 183

Chapter 10: Nine Steps We Can Take Tomorrow 186

Section: 1. The Next Twenty Years in One Page 186

Section 2. Step 1 – Take Back Your Money 188

Section: 3. Step 2 – Buy the Building 190

Section: 4. Step 3 – Make Your Workplace an Ownership Place 193

Section: 5. Step 4 – Secure the Land for the Next Generation 196

Section: 6. Step 5 – Refuse Predatory Finance 198

Section: 7. Step 6 – Start or Join One Cooperative Enterprise 201

Section: 8. Step 7 – Teach the Children a Trade They Can Own 203

Section: 9. Step 8 – Change the Laws That Still Can Be Changed 206

Section: 10. Step 9 – Form the New Guilds 208

Author's Final Note 211

Call to Action 214

About the Author 215

Glossary 216

Bibliography 219

Introduction

It is a Tuesday evening in the year 2026. A young father comes home from his second shift, shoes still dusted with warehouse concrete. His wife is at the kitchen table, laptop glowing, finishing charts for a client whose name she has never spoken aloud. Their three children are asleep on the couch because the second bedroom is now an office and the rent just went up again. On the counter sits a letter from the landlord: another eight percent "market adjustment." The father opens the banking app on his phone. The balance reads $312. He closes it without letting his wife see the screen.

They are not lazy. They are not stupid. They are not especially unlucky.

They are normal.

And normal, in our time, has become a slow-motion disaster.

You already know the statistics because you live them. The average new house now costs eight times the average household income; in 1980 it cost three. Sixty-three percent of American adults say they could not cover an unexpected $400 bill without borrowing or selling something. The bottom half of the country owns less than one percent of corporate stock; the top ten percent owns ninety-three. We have the most productive economy in human history, and the typical man in his thirties has less wealth than his father did at the same age.

Meanwhile the two loudest voices in the room keep shouting the same exhausted lines:

On one side: "The market will fix it. Just learn to code, launch a start-up, invest in crypto, hustle harder." On the other side: "The market is rigged. Let the state take over health care, housing, child-rearing, everything. Only a bigger bureaucracy can save you."

Both answers assume the same thing: ordinary families will never own anything that matters. One side calls that freedom. The other side calls it justice. Both sides are killing us.

There is a third voice, almost forgotten, that says something different:

Every normal family should own enough productive property to live in decency and independence, without being crushed by debt or managed by bureaucrats. Not luxury. Not utopia. Just the normal human minimum.

That voice has a name most people have never heard: distributism. It is not new. It is older than capitalism and older than Marx. It is rooted in the Book of Deuteronomy, the Gospels, the medieval guilds, the American homestead acts, and the cooperative empires that quietly thrive in corners of Europe right now. It was defended by popes, Anglican poets, Southern farmers, and Basque priests. It has never been fairly tried at any scale that would let us judge it. And it has never been more relevant than tonight.

This book is written for the father staring at the $312 balance. It is written for his wife who wonders if they will ever stop renting someone else's future. It is written for their children, who deserve to inherit something more than subscriptions and student loans.

We will not insult you with slogans or nostalgia. We will show, step by step, why capitalism and socialism are two sides of the same servile coin; why both of them, in practice, concentrate ownership and dissolve the family; and why a civilization of widespread property is not only just and beautiful, but possible, practical, and already working in fragments all over the world.

The prophets of despair tell us the household is obsolete. We intend to prove that the household is the revolution we are waiting for.

If you have ever lain awake wondering how your children will ever afford a life that is not borrowed, this book is for you. If you have ever felt that neither political party actually cares whether normal families own anything, this book is for you. If you believe that Christianity has something deeper to say about economics than "render unto Caesar and hope for the best," this book is for you.

Chapter 1: The False Dichotomy

Section: 1. The Cage-Fight That Ate the Century

Imagine a boxing ring set up in the middle of history.

In the red corner: Capitalism, sleek and confident, promising that if you just let the market work, everyone will eventually get rich. In the blue corner: Socialism, stern, idealistic, promising that if the people seize the means of production, no one will ever be poor again.

For a hundred and fifty years the two fighters have hammered each other senseless. Blood on the canvas, headlines every night, crowds roaring. The bell rings in 1848 with *The Communist Manifesto*. The fight goes global in 1917. It staggers through the Depression, turns apocalyptic in the 1940s, and finally, in 1989, the blue fighter collapses against the ropes. The referee raises the red fighter's hand. The crowd goes wild. "History is over," someone shouts.

And yet, quietly, both fighters limp to the same dressing room and split the purse.

Because here is the secret nobody announced over the loudspeaker: while the audience was busy picking sides, the promoters (big capital and big state) had agreed on one non-negotiable rule: ordinary families must never be allowed to own enough productive property to live independently of the ring. One fighter wanted that property concentrated in private hands, the other in bureaucratic hands. Neither wanted it distributed to millions of households. On that single point they were in perfect agreement and still are.

So the red corner won the match on points, but the promoters kept the prize.

Today the blue fighter is back on his feet (younger, louder, rebranded as "democratic socialism"), and half the crowd is cheering for a rematch. The other half insists the red fighter just needs to take off the gloves entirely ("unleash markets, deregulate everything"). Almost nobody notices that both fighters are still wearing the same promoter's logo on their trunks.

Meanwhile, out in the parking lot, the family from the Introduction is trying to figure out how to stretch $312 until next Friday.

They do not care who wins the fight. They only want to know why, after a century and a half of world-historic combat, they still do not own anything that produces wealth while they sleep. Why the ring is bigger than ever, the tickets more expensive, and the exits locked from the outside.

The answer is painfully simple: the fight itself was the distraction.

As long as we all kept our eyes on the two sweating giants in the center of the ring, almost no one noticed the third door at the back of the arena. The one that was quietly bricked up in the nineteenth century and has stayed bricked up ever since.

This book is about what lies behind that door, why it matters more in 2026 than it did in 1926, and how we can tear the bricks out with our bare hands if we have to.

But first we have to admit we have been watching the wrong show.

Section: 2. "Private vs. State": The Question That Was Never the Real Question

Suppose you walk into a village and discover that the only well has been bought by a single man who now sells water by the bucket. Some villagers argue that the well should stay in private hands ("private ownership is more efficient"). Others insist the village council must seize the well and distribute water for free ("state ownership is more just").

Both sides shout, march, write manifestos. Both sides are missing the prior question: why should one man, or one committee, control the only source of water in the first place?

The real question is not "private or state?" The real question is "owned by how many, and for the sake of what?"

The capitalism–socialism debate has spent a century and a half arguing about the color of the padlock on the well while quietly accepting that ninety-nine percent of the village will never hold a key.

Capitalism says: "Let one gifted entrepreneur own the well; his profit motive will make water cheaper in the long run." Socialism says: "Let the state own the well; its compassion will make water free in the long run." Both answers assume the villagers themselves must remain permanent customers, dependent either on a corporation's pricing algorithm or a bureaucrat's five-year plan.

Distributism walks up to the same well and asks an older, simpler question: "Why can't every household have its own rain barrel, its own cistern, its own small share in a community borehole?" Not because technology is lacking (it isn't), and not because human nature is too selfish, but because the legal and financial structures built over the last two centuries have been deliberately designed to make that outcome either illegal or impossible.

The tradition from Aristotle to Aquinas to the medieval guilds to the papal encyclicals never accepted the private–state framing. For them, property had three legitimate modes:

- Personal goods (your clothes, your toothbrush)
- Family or household goods (the farm, the workshop, the tools that feed your children)
- Common goods (rivers, forests, village pastures held in trust for all)

The middle term (property attached to the family or small association) was considered the normal, healthy state of affairs. Widespread ownership of productive assets was treated as the default, not the exception.

When ownership drifts too far toward the one (monopoly, oligarchy) or toward the many-managed-by-one (state socialism), society becomes unstable, unfree, and eventually inhuman.

The 19th century simply erased the middle term from the conversation. Capitalism declared it inefficient. Socialism declared it bourgeois. Both declared it impossible.

And so the well stayed locked, the argument stayed loud, and the village stayed thirsty.

The next section will show exactly how that erasure happened (and who profited from it).

Section: 3. How the Dichotomy Was Forged

The bricking-up of the third door did not happen by accident. It happened in four brutal centuries ago, and we are still living inside the wall.

The False Dichotomy of Capitalism and Socialism: A Christian Alternative

Beat 1 – The Great Dispossession (15th–18th centuries) In 1500, roughly half the land in England was owned by villages in common or by yeoman farmers working small freeholds. By 1850, almost none of it was. The Enclosure Acts (more than 5,000 separate laws passed between 1604 and 1914) turned millions of acres of commons, meadows, and small farms into large private estates. Villagers who had grazed a cow or gathered firewood for centuries were suddenly "trespassers." Result: a new creature appeared—the landless wage laborer. For the first time in history, large numbers of men had no choice but to sell their labor by the day or the hour. The industrial revolution did not create that class; it merely inherited it.

Beat 2 – The Promise of Wages in Exchange for Ownership (late 18th–19th centuries) Classical economics stepped forward with a soothing story: "Yes, you have lost your land, your tools, your independence. But fear not. The factory will pay wages, and wages will be your new property." Adam Smith, David Ricardo, and John Stuart Mill—all of them assumed that wages could permanently substitute for ownership. They treated widespread productive property as a quaint pre-modern relic, like the spinning wheel. The wager was simple: give up three acres and a cow, and in return you will get a steady paycheck, cheap bread, and eventually a suburban comfort. Two centuries later we can say with confidence: the wager was lost.

Beat 3 – The Socialist Counter-Wager (1848 onward) Marx and his heirs looked at the same dispossessed workers and drew the opposite conclusion: the problem was not that ownership had been taken away, but that it had been taken by the wrong people. Their solution: take it from the capitalists and hand it to the state, which would act as trustee for everyone. Notice the shared premise: productive property must be concentrated—either in a few private hands or in one public hand. The idea that it could be de-concentrated, divided again among millions of households, was dismissed as reactionary peasant fantasy.

Beat 4 – The 20th-Century Truce (1945–present) After the horrors of the Second World War and the Cold War, the exhausted West struck a compromise: let private monopolies keep most of the capital, and let the state tax them heavily to provide welfare, public education, and pensions. This "mixed economy" was sold as the reasonable middle way. In reality it was the final triumph of the dichotomy: capital remained concentrated, the welfare state grew gigantic, and the ordinary family still did not own the machines, the land, or the code that actually produce wealth. We just swapped the harsh landlord for the softer landlord who sends the cheque on the first of the month.

Four centuries, four steps, one result: the third door (the one marked "property for the many") was first dismantled, then ridiculed, then forgotten.

But doors, once bricked up, can still be reopened. The bricks were laid by men; they can be removed by men.

Next we will uncover the one thing both sides quietly agreed on—and why that agreement is now collapsing under its own contradictions.

Section: 4. The Secret Agreement Beneath the Noise

Everyone thinks capitalism and socialism hate each other. They do, but only the way rival gangsters hate each other: loudly, violently, and always while protecting the same street.

The street has a name: the gangsters never say out loud: The Separation of the Many from Productive Property.

Listen to the founders speak for themselves (side by side, for once):

Adam Smith (1776) "Civil government, so far as it is instituted for the security of property, is in reality instituted for the defence of the rich against the poor, or of those who have some property against those who have none at all."

Karl Marx (1867) "The theory of the Communists may be summed up in the single sentence: Abolition of private property." (He meant, of course, private property in the means of production.)

Friedrich Hayek (1944) "The system of private property is the most important guarantee of freedom, not only for those who own property, but scarcely less for those who do not." (Translation: freedom is safe because the propertyless still have the theoretical right to become owners someday.)

Modern technocrat (2023, World Economic Forum panel) "You'll own nothing, and you'll be happy."

Notice the pattern. Whether the speaker is celebrating the market, the revolution, or the subscription economy, the ordinary household is never imagined as an owner of anything serious. At best it is a consumer, at worst a ward of the state, but never a proprietor.

Both systems require the same human material: millions of families who wake up every morning needing to rent their labor (or beg for benefits) because they do not possess land, tools, machines, code, or equity that can feed them without permission.

Capitalism needs them insecure enough to accept any wage. Socialism needs them insecure enough to welcome any bureaucrat.

Both therefore wage quiet war on anything that would make families secure without them:

- Capitalism fights homestead laws, employee ownership, and restrictive zoning that would let people build wealth outside the stock market.
- Socialism fights inheritance, family businesses, and every attempt to keep productive wealth inside households rather than the state.

The proof is in the numbers nobody on either side wants to discuss:

- In 1989 (the supposed final victory of capitalism) the bottom 50 % of Americans owned 3.7 % of the nation's wealth.
- In 2024 they own 2.5 %.
- In the same period, the most "socialistic" countries in Europe (Sweden, Denmark) saw similar or greater concentrations at the very top.

The cage-fight was real, but the outcome was rigged from the beginning.

The family in your living room did not lose because they picked the wrong fighter. They lost because both fighters were paid to make sure families like theirs never leave the stands and step into the ring as owners.

Which brings us to the present moment, when the truce is cracking and the secret agreement is finally visible to hide.

Section: 5. The Human Cost of the Truce

Competition, rightly understood, is a good and necessary thing. It spurs innovation, rewards diligence, reveals what people truly value, and prevents stagnation. The early promise of capitalism rightly celebrated this: break old monopolies, let people trade freely, and ordinary families could rise through honest effort and ingenuity. Markets, when kept at a human scale, have repeatedly shown they can raise living standards far better than centralized planning.

In many cases, think of the vigorous rivalry among small family firms in Taiwan's machine-tool districts or the networked co-ops of Emilia-Romagna. Competition at the human scale has driven remarkable creativity and resilience without creating a new aristocracy of owners.

The problem arises when competition is allowed, or encouraged, to become winner-take-most. When legal structures, tax policy, zoning, intellectual property rules, and access to patient capital favor scale above all else, the invisible hand begins to favor the already large. Small owners get squeezed not because they are less efficient, but because the game is tilted toward concentration. As economist Alexander Salter argues in *The Political Economy of Distributism*, distributism does not reject markets or competition. It insists they must be embedded in institutions that keep ownership dispersed, so that competition serves human flourishing rather than devouring it. Healthy competition thrives when there are many players with real skin in the game, family workshops, worker co-ops, and independent farms, not when a handful of giants can buy up or regulate out their rivals.

Distributism, then, is not anti-market. It is pro-competition in the service of widespread property. It wants the kind of vigorous rivalry that medieval guilds and modern Taiwanese SMEs have shown is possible, while guarding against the servile outcome Belloc warned about. Markets are powerful tools, but like fire, they need a hearth. Otherwise they burn the house down.

Go back to the family we met in the Introduction.

It is now the first week of November 2026. The rent increase has been paid (by putting groceries on a credit card). The father took extra shifts at the warehouse; the mother took an overnight proofreading gig. Their eight-year-old asked why they never go to the park anymore. They could not bring themselves to say, "Because we both have to work on Saturdays now."

This is not a sob story. This is the new normal for the majority.

Both victors of the great 20th-century fight promised this family something better.

Capitalism promised: "Work hard, play by the rules, and the ladder of upward mobility will always be there." The ladder is now mostly gone. The rungs that remain are greased. In 1980 a single median income could buy a median house, support a stay-at-home parent, and still save 10 % for retirement. Today two above-median incomes barely cover rent, childcare, health insurance, and student debt.

Socialism (or its softer social-democratic versions) promised a safety net so generous that ownership would become unnecessary. The net is real, but it is strung lower every year. In the United States, the real value of welfare benefits for a family of four has fallen 20 % since 2000. In Europe, the celebrated Nordic model now requires 85–90 % female workforce participation and taxes so high that young couples postpone children until their late thirties (if they have them at all).

Both systems kept their deepest promise: the family remains dependent.

The spiritual damage is harder to measure, but you feel it every day:

- A father who cannot say "bring home the bacon" because bacon now requires two incomes and a side hustle.
- A mother who cannot be home with her toddlers because the mortgage will not pay itself.
- Children who grow up believing that adulthood means scanning a badge for someone else's profit until you are too worn out to enjoy the years you have left.
- Marriages quietly suffocating under money anxiety that never sleeps.

Fertility rates across the developed world have crashed below replacement, not primarily because people hate children, but because they cannot imagine giving a child the economic security they themselves never had.

The promoters call this "creative destruction" or "late-capitalism" or "late-stage capitalism" or "necessary transition." The family in the living room calls it Tuesday.

And here is the cruelest part: the same voices that spent a century shouting at each other about justice and freedom now shrug and say there is no alternative.

But there was. There still is. And it was never defeated in open debate; it was simply shouted down by louder, richer men who needed the fight to continue.

The next section will show you the moment when the Church herself stepped into the ring, pointed to the bricked-up door, and said, "That one. Open that one." Almost nobody listened then. We can listen now.

Section: 6. The Door They Bricked Up

In 1891, while the promoters were still busy selling tickets to the cage-fight, an old man in Rome opened a window and shouted into the arena.

His name was Leo XIII. His message was short enough to fit on a single page, yet it terrified both corners of the ring.

Rerum Novarum, paragraph 46–47:

"The law, therefore, should favor ownership, and its policy should be to induce as many as possible of the people to become owners… If working people can be encouraged to look forward to obtaining a share in the land, or in the business they work for, the gulf between vast wealth and sheer poverty will be bridged… A working man's little estate, acquired by toil and thrift, is a far more effective safeguard of family life than any amount of state aid."

Translation: every normal family should own something that produces wealth. Not as charity. Not as a government handout. As justice.

Forty years later, in the middle of the Great Depression, Pius XI went further. Quadragesimo Anno (1931), paragraph 59–63, explicitly endorsed what he called the "distributist" order: capital and tools should be spread as widely as possible, so that the worker is not a wage-slave to a private master nor a serf to the state, but a co-owner with real responsibility and real freedom.

He even praised guilds, cooperatives, and family-sized enterprises as the concrete forms this order could take.

These were not side remarks. They were the official reply of the Catholic Church to the entire 19th-century quarrel. And they were ignored the quarrel's central premise. They refused to choose between the red corner and the blue corner. They pointed to the third door and said, "Walk through there."

The reaction?

Capitalists called it "medieval nostalgia." Socialists called it "papal fascism." Politicians on both sides quietly filed the documents under "harmless religious opinion" and went back to the fight.

The encyclicals were translated, printed, and promptly shelved. The promoters kept selling tickets. The bricks stayed in place.

Yet the door itself never disappeared. It is still there, behind the wall, perfectly intact.

And in the last twenty years something new has happened: the wall has begun to crack on its own. The cage-fight is running out of money and out of believers. People who have never heard of Leo XIII or Pius XI are starting to ask the forbidden question again: "Why can't regular families own things that make money?"

That question is the sound of the first brick falling.

The next section will show you how to pull the rest down.

Section: 7. Breaking Out of the Cage

The fight is fixed. The crowd is exhausted. The promoters are counting money in a back room while the two battered boxers pretend to hate each other for the cameras.

But the arena is not the world. It is only a building, and every building has more than one door.

One of those doors was bricked up two centuries ago by men who needed you landless, tool-less, equity-less, and therefore obedient. Tonight the mortar is crumbling.

You do not need to wait for a revolution. You do not need to beg the red corner or the blue corner for permission. You only need to notice that the third door is still there, unmarked, unlit, but structurally sound, and that millions of other tired families are already putting their shoulders to it.

In the pages ahead we will walk through that door together. We will meet the families (past and present) who already live on the other side. We will see the tools they use, the laws they changed, the businesses they own, the children they raise without selling their lives by the hour.

And we will discover something that should have been obvious all along:

The opposite of servitude is not leisure. The opposite of servitude is ownership.

When enough households own again, the cage-fight will not end with a bang or a negotiation. It will simply run out of spectators.

Chapter 2: The Human Scale

Section:1. The Creature Who Needs a Garden

In the beginning, God did not give Adam a job application. He gave him a garden.

"Be fruitful and multiply," yes; but the very next words are: "fill the earth and subdue it… The Lord God took the man and put him in the garden of Eden to work it and keep it." Before a single commandment is spoken about sin, sacrifice, or even worship, the Bible records that the normal human state is to have something real to tend, defend, and pass on.

A garden is not an investment portfolio. A garden is not a government program. A garden is dirt under the fingernails, seasons you can taste, fruit you can pick with your child on your shoulders. It is property that feeds both body and soul, property that demands responsibility and rewards it with independence.

This is the first economic act in Scripture: God makes a creature and immediately gives him a productive asset proportionate to his strength and his dignity. Not too little, not too much, but exactly enough for a free life.

Every attempt since then to reorganize human society without that original gift has produced monsters.

Take the garden away and give the man a cubicle forty hours a week: he becomes restless, sick, and strangely ashamed. Take the garden away and give him a welfare check: he becomes listless, bored, and still ashamed. Leave the garden in place and he sings while he works, teaches his son the names of the trees, and brings the first tomato of the season to the widow next door without being taxed or managed into it.

The entire Bible, from Genesis to Revelation, can be read as the story of a God who refuses to give up on the dream that His children should once again walk in a garden they can call their own.

The modern world thinks that dream is sentimental. God thinks it is the definition of justice.

We begin here, with the mud between Adam's toes, because if we get the creature wrong we will get the economy wrong. Man is not an infinitely scalable labor unit. He is not a consumption node in a global supply chain. He is a gardener who has forgotten he was ever given a garden, and the ache you feel at 2 a.m. when the rent is due is the homesickness of a dispossessed son.

The good news is that gardens can be planted again. The next pages will show you what the great tradition has always known: the human scale is not a quaint option. It is the only scale at which a human being can be fully human.

Section: 2. Aristotle's Forgotten Sentence

Most people who quote Aristotle on property quote the wrong part.

They love to repeat that "man is by nature a political animal," then skip straight to Plato's communism or Hobbes's war of all against all. But tucked inside the Politics (Book II, chapter 5) is a single sentence so explosive that every subsequent revolution has tried to pretend it was never written:

"Property should be in a general sense common, but as a general rule private; for when everyone has a distinct interest, men will not complain of one another, and they will make more progress, because everyone will be attending to his own business."

Read it slowly.

Aristotle is not defending the sacred rights of billionaires. He is also not defending collectivization. He is saying the natural, peace-producing, progress-producing state of affairs is when most productive property is privately owned by the people who actually use it, while remaining morally ordered to the common good.

In the same passage he warns against two equal and opposite errors:

- Too much concentration ("when property belongs to a few, the many are inevitably discontented").
- Too much collectivization ("when property is held in common, the diligent resent the lazy, and everything falls into neglect").

His solution is neither monopoly nor commune, but widespread distribution. Every citizen (and by extension every household) should have "a distinct interest," a plot, a workshop, a herd, a vineyard, something whose fruits he can see and taste and hand to his children.

Why? Because only then does work feel like stewardship instead of servitude. Only then does the future feel like inheritance instead of roulette. Only then does the city enjoy both peace and prosperity.

Aristotle wrote this 2,300 years before Chesterton or Belloc, before the papal encyclicals, before anyone had heard the word "distributism." Yet he already saw the entire argument in one clean stroke:

Human beings flourish when ownership is private enough for responsibility and common enough for fraternity.

Everything since has been footnotes, most of them written by people trying to erase that sentence.

The Philosopher did not think this was utopian. He thought it was the only arrangement compatible with human nature as God (or the gods) actually made it.

We forgot the sentence. The 19th century buried it under factories and favelas. The 20th century drowned it in manifestos and mortgages.

But nature does not forget. And the homesick gardener inside every modern wage-slave still remembers the taste of fruit he grew himself.

Next we will watch St. Thomas take Aristotle's sentence, baptize it, and turn it into the quiet engine of a thousand years of Christian civilization.

Section: 3. Thomas Aquinas and the Family as the First Economy

St. Thomas never wrote a treatise called "On Distributism." He didn't need to. Every time he opens his mouth about property, distributism walks out fully dressed.

Start with the single most important line in the entire Summa Theologiae on this topic (II-II, Question 66, Article 2):

"It is lawful for a man to possess something as his own… Moreover, in human life the principal thing is the sustenance of life, and for this external goods are necessary. Therefore it is necessary that some things be possessed by men as their own."

Translation: owning productive property is not a luxury. It is part of the natural law written into the human condition of being a flesh-and-blood creature who must eat, marry, and raise children.

Now watch what he does next (Article 7):

"Community of goods is said to be part of the natural law, not because natural law dictates that all things should be possessed in common and nothing privately, but because the distinction of property is not by natural law, but rather by the addition of human reason… Yet this distinction was introduced for the benefit of human life."

In plain English: private property is not a regrettable concession to sin. It is a positive invention of reason that makes human life more peaceful and more fruitful than any commune could ever be.

But here is the part no one teaches in economics class (Article 1 and 2 again):

The purpose of private property is to secure the family. Not the individual. Not the corporation. Not the state. The family.

Thomas quotes Aristotle approvingly: things are better cared for when each person has his own to tend. Then he adds the decisive Christian twist: the "person" who most needs to tend and be secure is not the lone bachelor, but the father and mother who must feed children for eighteen years with no guarantee of tomorrow's wages.

Therefore the default subject of property rights over productive property is the household, not the individual investor or the bureaucratic office.

Whatever can be worked by a family or a small band of families and still support them in decency, whether a farm, a workshop, a fishing boat, a bakery, or a software co-op, belongs by the logic of creation and redemption in their hands first.

When Thomas says a man may lawfully own "quantum sufficit ad vitam sustentandam" (as much as suffices for the sustenance of life), he is not talking about a 401(k) or a stock portfolio. He is talking about the amount of land, tools, or capital that lets a man look his children in the eye and say, "As long as God gives me strength, no one will take this roof or this table from us."

That is why he treats permanent dispossession (the deliberate creation of a propertyless proletariat) as a form of violence against nature itself.

The Angelic Doctor never saw a factory, a hedge fund, or a Marxist. Yet in eight calm pages he dismantled the intellectual foundations of both Walmart and the Kremlin.

He simply asked: What kind of ownership does a human family need in order to live a fully human life? Then he answered with the quiet, unstoppable logic: enough to be free, not so much as to oppress, and always ordered to the common good.

Everything Christian civilization built for the next seven centuries (guilds, commons, family farms, craft shops, monastic estates) was nothing more than that logic made visible in wood, stone, and soil.

We tore it down in four centuries. We can rebuild it in one. But only if we remember who the real owner was meant to be: not the lone entrepreneur, not the faceless state, but the families that sleep under one roof and calls itself a home.

Section: 4. Martin Luther and the Household Economy (Oeconomia)

A generation and a half after Thomas, another voice gave these truths a powerful Reformation shape. Martin Luther stood firmly in the same broad Christian tradition. At the same time he recovered the plain sense of Scripture and the dignity of ordinary vocation.

Luther did not write a formal treatise called "On Distributism." Yet every time he spoke of daily bread, honest work, or the orders God instituted for human life, the same vision emerged. Most families should possess enough productive property to live in responsible freedom, stewardship, and service to neighbor.

Luther taught that God governs human life through three estates or hierarchies: the ecclesia (the church), the politia (civil government), and the oeconomia (the household economy). The oeconomia is not a mere consumer unit. It is the God-ordained realm in which parents provide for their children, exercise stewardship over land and tools, and serve their neighbors through faithful vocation. Marriage, family, farming, crafting, and honest buying and selling all belong here. The household is where most Christians live out their calling day by day. It requires real, productive assets if it is to fulfill its divine purpose.

Luther defended private property vigorously against radical communal experiments. Property is a gift from God for the sustenance of life and the exercise of love. Yet he condemned with equal force the spirit of unlimited profit-seeking, usury, and monopoly that was already beginning to dispossess ordinary families in his day. In his 1524 treatise *On Trade and Usury*, he denounced merchants who bought up entire commodities in order to control supply and fix prices. He said they acted as if the creatures and goods of God were created for them alone. Such practices, he warned, open every window and door to hell. They turn the market into a tool of avarice rather than mutual service. Buying and selling must remain subordinate to the needs of households and the common good, not driven by the logic of maximum gain.

For Luther, as for the medieval village and the biblical Jubilee, the normal Christian economic order is one in which families have enough land, tools, or workshop to provide daily bread without perpetual dependence on wages or bureaucrats. Work in the oeconomia is dignified vocation, not servile drudgery. The father who can look his children in the eye and say, "This field or this forge or this trade is ours by God's gift and our labor" is living in the freedom for which Christ has set us free.

Luther never saw the full industrial revolution or modern corporations. Yet in his fierce defense of the household against early forms of concentrated capital and his elevation of ordinary work as holy calling, he retrieved and applied the same ancient Christian conviction we find in Aquinas. Productive property exists first for families, not for the few or the state. He stood with the gardener in Eden and the small owners of the medieval strips. He reminded us that man was not made to be a landless wage-laborer, nor a ward of the state, but a steward with something real to tend, defend, and pass on.

Section: 5. The Sabbath Pattern Written Into Creation

Every seventh day God commanded the impossible: Stop producing. Let the land lie fallow. Let the ox rest. Let the servant rest. Let even the foreigner who happens to be inside your gates rest.

Then, every seventh year, He commanded something even more impossible: Cancel debts. Let slaves go free. Let the soil breathe.

And every fiftieth year (the Jubilee), the most impossible of all: Return every family to its ancestral land. Whatever had been bought, sold, foreclosed, or conquered must go back to the household that originally worked it.

Modern ears hear these laws and think "poetic idealism." God meant them as the way an engineer means blueprints.

The Sabbath laws are not a religious add-on to economics. They are the operating system.

Notice what the laws assume:

- Most families will normally own productive property (land, animals, tools); otherwise "return the land" would be meaningless.
- Debt must never become permanent servitude; otherwise "cancel debts" would be cruel mockery.
- The soil itself has rights; otherwise letting it rest every seventh year would be economic suicide.

In other words, the entire Torah economy is built for a nation of small owners who work with their hands, owe little, and can actually afford to obey God by stopping work.

This is not socialism: the land is not nationalized; it is stubbornly, fiercely private ("the land shall not be sold in perpetuity, for the land is Mine," says the Lord, and you are only tenants). This is not capitalism: the market may not permanently alienate a family property; every transaction is provisional until the trumpet of the Jubilee.

The Sabbath pattern is distributism in the raw.

It protects the family from two equal and opposite disasters:

- From the rich creditor who would turn a bad harvest into permanent dispossession.
- From the lazy debtor who would live forever on borrowed money.

Every seven years the scales are reset so that no family is crushed forever and no family is rewarded forever for idleness.

The result is a society in which ownership is widespread, debt is temporary, and rest is possible.

When Israel forgot the Sabbath and the Jubilee, the prophets did not thunder about sexual immorality first. They thundered about land concentration first.

Isaiah 5: "Woe to you who join house to house, who add field to field, until there is no more room, and you are made to dwell alone in the midst of the land." Amos 8: "Buying the poor for silver and the needy for a pair of sandals." Micah 2: "They covet fields and seize them, and houses, and take them away; they oppress a man and his house, a man and his inheritance."

The great sin of Israel was not idolatry in the abstract. It was the creation of a propertyless class.

God's answer was never to collectivize the land. It was to restore every family to its plot every fifty years.

We treat the Jubilee as a charming footnote. God treated it as the heartbeat of justice.

The early Church did not repeal that heartbeat; she simply universalized it. In Christ the ultimate debt was cancelled once for all, and the ultimate inheritance was restored. But the pattern remained: Christians are to live in the world as people who have received an inheritance they did not earn and must pass on undiminished.

The Sabbath, the Sabbatical Year, and the Jubilee are not "Old Testament laws we don't keep anymore." They are the permanent protest of the Creator against every economy that makes rest impossible for the many and ownership impossible for the poor.

They are God's way of saying: "My children were not made to run on a treadmill forever. They were made to work six days and then walk in the garden with Me on the seventh."

Any economic order that cannot deliver that seventh day to ordinary families is already under prophetic judgment.

Next we will see how the first Christians actually lived that pattern (and why the usual accusations of "early Christian communism" are the exact opposite of the truth).

Section: 6. "Neither Mine Nor Thine, But Ours": Acts 2 and 4 Read Correctly

Every few years someone discovers Acts 2:44–45 and Acts 4:32–35 and shouts, "See! The early Church was communist!"

Then someone else shouts back, "No, it was voluntary charity, not communism!"

Both are wrong.

Read the texts slowly, in Greek if you can, in English if you must, but read them as if you had never heard the capitalism–socialism shouting match.

Acts 2:44–45 "All who believed were together and had all things in common. And they were selling their possessions and belongings and distributing the proceeds to all, as any had need."

Acts 4:32–35 "Now the full number of those who believed were of one heart and soul, and no one said that any of the things that belonged to him was his own, but they had everything in common… There was not a needy person among them, for as many as were owners of lands or houses sold them and brought the proceeds… and it was distributed to each as any had need."

Notice what is not there:

- No decree from the apostles ordering liquidation of property.
- No state or collective seizing anything.
- No threat of punishment for keeping your farm.

Now notice what is there:

- The word "owners" (κύριοι τῶν κτημάτων ἢ τῶν οἰκιῶν) appears in 4:34. They sold property they still legally owned.
- Peter's devastating line to Ananias in Acts 5:4: "While it remained unsold, did it not remain your own? And after it was sold, was it not at your disposal?"

Translation: private ownership was intact before the sale, private ownership of the money intact after the sale. Ananias and Sapphira died not for keeping property, but for lying about a gift they had freely chosen to make.

What actually happened in Jerusalem was not communism. It was something far more radical: perfect Christian freedom producing perfect Christian generosity, built on top of secure private ownership.

The early Christians did not abolish property. They abolished need.

Because they were owners (of land, houses, money), they could choose to sell and give. Because the choice was truly free, the gift was truly beautiful. Because the gift was so beautiful, there was not a needy person among them.

This is the exact opposite of the servile state. In the servile state you are compelled to give everything and still remain needy. In the early Church you were free to keep everything yet chose to make sure no one was needy.

The sequence matters:

1. Secure ownership →
2. Radical freedom →
3. Voluntary superabundance →
4. No one in need.

Reverse the sequence (start with compulsion) and you get resentment, inefficiency, and eventually gulags.

The Jerusalem community was the Sabbath economy breaking into history: a society of owners who loved one another so much that ownership stopped feeling like a wall and started feeling like a bridge.

It was never meant to be a permanent civil constitution (the Church quickly spread into cultures where mass land-sales were impossible). It was meant to be a sign: "This is what human community looks like when the Holy Spirit is poured out on people who are already free."

Every monastery, every religious order, every parish food pantry that actually works is still living from that sign.

And every modern attempt to achieve the same result by confiscation rather than conversion has produced the opposite: universal poverty of goods and universal poverty of soul.

The early Church was not "communist." It was distributist perfection: every believer an owner, every owner a cheerful giver, and therefore no one in need.

That is the pattern we are still called to imitate, not with five-year plans or hedge funds, but with converted hearts and restored households.

Next we will watch Jesus Himself tell a story about property that every Sunday-school child knows, yet almost no economist has ever understood.

Section: 7. The Parable of the Talents as Distributist Manifesto

Most of us heard the Parable of the Talents as children and came away with a safe moral: "Use your gifts or lose them." That is true, but it is the children's version.

Read it again as adults (Matthew 25:14–30) and something far more revolutionary appears.

A wealthy master is going on a journey. He does not give his property to one trusted manager. He does not hand it to a committee of the whole. He calls his own servants (three ordinary men) and distributes the capital to them personally, "to each according to his ability": eight talents to one, five to another, two to the last man one single talent.

Then he leaves.

No daily reports. No micromanagement. No state audit. Just capital in the hands of the people who will actually use it, and a simple command: "Trade with these until I come."

When the master returns, he does not ask, "How big is the total fund now?" He asks each man, face to face, "What did you do with what I gave you?"

The man with five talents turned them into ten. The man with two turned them into four. Both hear the same astonishing words: "Well done, good and faithful servant… Enter into the joy of your master."

The man with one talent buried it. He is condemned not for being poor, not for failing to become rich, but for refusing to act like an owner.

Now step back and notice what the parable quietly assumes:

- Productive capital is meant to be distributed, not concentrated.
- It is distributed to many small stewards, not to one super-manager or one central bureau.
- Each steward is judged by increase, not by equality of outcome.
- The master wants multiplication, not preservation; risk and creativity are praised.
- The servant who treats capital as something that belongs only to the distant master (and therefore buries it) is cast out as "wicked and slothful."

In ten short verses Jesus sketches an economy that is neither capitalist nor socialist:

- Capital is widely distributed ("to each").

- Ownership carries real responsibility and real freedom.
- Inequality of talents is accepted as natural ("according to his ability").
- The goal is fruitful stewardship, not mere security or equal shares.
- The one sin that cannot be tolerated is the refusal to exercise ownership.

This is not the parable of the hedge fund. This is the parable of the family farm, the guild workshop, the worker co-op, the small software studio, the homestead with a few acres and a lot of children.

It is the parable of every father who hands his son the keys to the tractor and says, "Make it grow." It is the parable of every daughter who takes the recipe book from her mother and opens a bakery on the corner.

The kingdom of heaven, says Jesus, is like a man who dared to make many small owners and then trusted them to act like it.

Modern capitalism concentrates the talents in one or two servants and calls that "efficiency." Modern socialism takes the talents back from all the servants and locks them in a government vault and calls that "justice." Both hear the master return and say, "Lord, I knew you were a hard man… so I buried what was yours."

And both, in the end, are cast into the outer darkness where there is weeping and gnashing of teeth.

The third way, the way of the kingdom, is the way almost no one tried: give the talents to the many, let them trade, let them multiply, let them feast.

That is the economy the Master smiles on.

That is the economy we are still invited to enter.

Next, for one shining moment in history, the world almost did.

Section: 8. The Medieval Synthesis in One Paragraph

Picture an ordinary English village in the year 1250, the hour just before sunrise.

The bell rings for Prime. A farmer steps out of his wattle-and-daub house carrying a wooden bowl still steaming with pottage. His wife follows with the baby slung on her hip; their two older boys are already driving the family's three cows toward the common meadow where every villager has the ancient right to graze a fixed number of beasts. On the way they pass the open fields divided into hundreds of narrow strips; the farmer's strips lie scattered among his neighbors' so that no one gets all the good soil or all the bad. By sunset he will have ploughed his own strips with his own oxen, but the oxen belong to the village plough-team to which every household contributes.

Across the lane the baker feeds his oven with faggots he collected from the lord's wood (a right called estovers, measured exactly so the wood never runs out). The miller, who owns the only mill, must grind the village grain at a fixed legal price and may take only one-twenty-fourth as his fee. The blacksmith's teenage son is apprenticed to the guild in the nearest town; when he finishes, he will return with the legal right to set up his own forge here. The priest farms his thirty-acre glebe with the help of the parish, and the tithe money keeps the church roof tight and the poor fed. The lord of the manor lives in the stone hall on the hill, but even he may not enclose the common pasture or evict a freeholder without breaking the custom of the manor, a custom older than his family and enforced by king's judges.

In this one square mile almost every household owns or co-owns something productive: land, animals, tools, rights in the commons, a place in the guild, a share in the mill's profits, a garden, an orchard, a loom in the corner. No one is rich by modern standards. No one is propertyless. No one works for wages unless he chooses to, and even the wage is usually paid in bread, ale, and a strip of rye. Debt exists, but it rarely lasts beyond seven years; the Church courts will cancel it sooner if it threatens a family's subsistence. Children learn trades beside their parents, not in distant factories. Festivals are frequent, work stops at dusk, and Sunday is truly the Lord's Day because most people can actually afford to keep it.

This was not utopia. There was plague, bad harvests, the occasional brutal lord. But for half a millennium this arrangement kept the vast majority of families fed, housed, skilled, and free in a way that no industrial society has ever matched. It was the Sabbath economy, the Jubilee spirit, the Aristotelian mean, and the Thomistic sufficiency all made flesh in one place.

Then the enclosures came, the guilds were suppressed, the commons were privatized into giant estates, and the villagers were turned into factory fodder or paupers. The third door slammed shut.

But the memory of that village did not die. It lived in the hearts of peasants who rioted against enclosure, in the encyclicals of popes, in the dreams of Englishmen named Chesterton and Spaniards named Arizmendi.

And it can live again.

Because the medieval synthesis was not a golden age that vanished. It was a working model of what happens when human beings are allowed to live at the human scale.

One more glimpse, and then we will bring the model home.

Next, the Scale that God Himself chose to become.

Section: 9. The Scale God Became

In the end, the strongest argument for the human scale is not a theory. It is a Person.

When the Second Person of the Trinity decided to join the creature He had made, He did not become a corporation, a non-profit, a government, or even a wandering philosopher-king. He became a baby.

A particular baby, born to a particular young woman and her carpenter husband, in a particular village of eight hundred souls, in a house that almost certainly contained a small woodworking shop where the daily bread was earned by human hands-on human-scale tools.

Nazareth was not a metaphor. It was a real place where real families owned small plots, paid taxes, argued about boundary stones, celebrated weddings that lasted a week, and buried their dead in tombs cut from the limestone hillside. The Holy Family lived on the proceeds of a family business. Joseph was not a wage employee of Nazareth Lumber Inc. He was a τέκτων—craftsman, builder, owner of his tools, setter of his hours, teacher of his trade to his foster Son.

For thirty years the Creator of galaxies submitted Himself to the scale of one village, one workshop, one mother who needed help carrying water from the well. He who measures the waters in the hollow of His hand allowed His own hands to be measured for a plane, a saw, a yoke.

If the infinite God judged the human scale sufficient for His own hidden life, then the human scale is sufficient for economics, for politics, for everything that matters.

He did not choose this scale because it was quaint. He chose it because it is the truth about us: we are finite creatures who become like Him most perfectly when we love, work, eat, pray, and die within reach of people who know our names.

Every economic order that makes such a life impossible for the majority is not merely inefficient; it is sacrilegious. Every economic order that makes it possible again is not merely practical; it is a participation in the Incarnation.

Chesterton once said that Christianity has not only discovered the dignity of the common man; it discovered the common man. The same faith that discovered the common man also discovered the common acre, the common workshop, the common table.

The God who became man did not do it to teach us nostalgia. He did it to teach us how to live.

The household republic is not a retreat from the world. It is the world restored to the size God always meant it to be: big enough for love, small enough for responsibility.

Lord, You who measured the universe with a span and then became a span-length infant in a borrowed stable: teach us again the measure of man. Make us small enough to fit the garden You first gave us, and bold enough to take it back. Amen.

We have seen what nature says, what revelation says, what philosophy and history say. Now it is time to meet the two men who, in the middle of the twentieth century's darkest hour, stood up and shouted the forgotten truth into a world that refused to listen.

Chapter 3: Chesterton and Belloc

Section: 1. Why We Are Reading Them Slowly

Consider the Shire. J.R.R. Tolkien, who loved the English countryside before the factories scarred it, gave us a vision of what widespread ownership once looked like and what it might look like again. He never wrote economic treatises, yet the Shire before its fall is distributism incarnate: a land of small freeholders, where most hobbits own their holes, their gardens, their mills, their fields of pipe-weed. Families live close to the earth they cultivate. Work is seasonal and sufficient, not endless extraction. Leisure, including feasting, storytelling, and pipe-smoking, is not a luxury but the natural fruit of enough property to rest without fear. Government is light, almost invisible. Tolkien writes, "hardly any," except for the occasional Sherriff to keep an eye on outsiders and the occasional tax on foreign goods. No monopolies swallow the mills. No state seizes the harvest "for fair distribution." Then the shadow falls. Saruman turns Isengard into a factory-hell. Trees are burned for bellows, rivers are choked with slag, and orcs are enslaved to machines. When that spirit reaches the Shire, the pattern repeats. Mills are industrialized, trees are felled, land is enclosed, and produce is confiscated by "gatherers and sharers" who promise equity but deliver tyranny. Both paths, ruthless efficiency for profit and ruthless efficiency for the collective, end in the same place: the household dispossessed, the land scarred, and beauty replaced by smoke. The Scouring is the answer distributism has always given. Ordinary hobbits, including gardeners, millers, and farmers, take back their homes. They do not wait for a king or a committee. They act as free men defending what is theirs. And when the ruffians are gone, the land heals. Trees are replanted, mills are repaired, and gardens are tended again by those who own them. Sam Gamgee returns to Bag End not as a tenant or a wage-earner, but as master of his own plot, husband to Rosie, and father to their children. The Shire blooms because its families once more hold the means to live in decency and independence. Tolkien did not need to name distributism. He showed it. He showed its loss and its recovery. He showed that when ordinary people lose their stake in the earth, the soul withers. When they reclaim it, the soul sings again.

Tolkien did not call himself a distributist, nor did he write treatises endorsing Belloc's specific remedies. He once described his politics as leaning toward "Anarchy (philosophically understood)" or "unconstitutional Monarchy." This was a vision of minimal interference, where authority is light, distant, and rooted in something higher than bureaucracy. Yet he was steeped in Chesterton and Belloc. Their ideas echoed in his imagination. The Shire is not a blueprint for their program, but it is a living portrait of what they hoped for: a society where families hold the means of life, and beauty endures because property is widespread and loved. Whether or not Tolkien signed the manifesto, he painted its fulfillment.

Most people who talk about Chesterton and Belloc have never read them. They know the slogans ("three acres and a cow," "the servile state") the way people know the chorus of a song without ever hearing the verses. The slogans are good, but they are only the froth on a very deep beer.

We are going to drink the beer. But first, note that this tradition of widespread ownership and the human scale is far older and broader than any single pair of writers. It is rooted in

Scripture itself—in the garden given to Adam, in the Jubilee laws of Leviticus, in the stewardship parables of Jesus, and in the Reformation recovery of vocation and the priesthood of all believers.

In the mid-twentieth century, the German Lutheran economist **Wilhelm Röpke** developed a powerful parallel vision he called the "humane economy." In works such as *A Humane Economy* (1958), Röpke drew on Reformed ethics and a deep reading of Scripture to advocate widespread small-scale ownership—family farms, independent craftsmen, and morally bounded markets—while fiercely opposing both totalitarian collectivism and dehumanizing monopoly capitalism. He insisted that a free economy must be embedded in strong families, local communities, and Christian moral order.

Röpke stands as a clear Protestant witness that the longing for a society of owners is not a Catholic peculiarity but a deeply Christian conviction. Similar themes appear in the Southern Agrarians of the 1930s, who defended the small farm and household economy against industrial gigantism, and in the Dutch Reformed statesman Abraham Kuyper's doctrine of sphere sovereignty, which guards the family and local associations from being swallowed by either the state or the corporation.

In the next pages we will do something old-fashioned: we will open two books (one published in 1912, one in 1926)

They answered with laughter, statistics, parables, and prophecy. Almost no one listened. The world chose the cage-fight instead.

In the next twenty pages we will do something old-fashioned: we will open two books (one published in 1912, one in 1926) and read ten specific pages of each as if no one had ever summarized, caricatured, or dismissed them before. We will read them slowly.

These are not polite suggestions from the Edwardian era. They are emergency dispatches from the future, written by two men who looked at the early twentieth century and saw, with terrifying clarity, the late twenty-first century we now inhabit.

They saw:

- the coming triumph of a handful of monopolies
- the disappearance of the independent shopkeeper and farmer
- the transformation of citizens into permanent employees or permanent welfare clients
- the quiet reintroduction of slavery under the new name "job security"

And they saw it all before the Russian Revolution had properly begun, before Henry Ford perfected the assembly line, before Amazon, BlackRock, or the iPhone existed.

They did not merely complain. They diagnosed the disease and prescribed the only remedy they believed could still work: the widest possible distribution of productive property to the greatest possible number of normal families.

Everyone else (liberals, socialists, conservatives, technocrats) told them it was impossible, nostalgic, Catholic, utopian, or all four. They answered with laughter, statistics, parables, and prophecy.

Almost no one listened. The world chose the cage-fight instead.

Yet here we are, a century later, living in the wreckage they predicted to the last detail.

So we are going to read them slowly, line by line, the way the first Christians read Paul's letters when the courier arrived from Corinth: not as museum pieces, but as living words that might still save us.

Section: 2. The Nine Best Pages of The Outline of Sanity (1926)

Open the book to Chapter IV, "A Misunderstanding about Method," and Chapter V, "A Misunderstanding about the Small Owner." Nine pages. Read them with me, slowly.

Chesterton begins with a confession that sounds almost flippant:

"I would give any one of them a cow, if anybody would teach him how to milk it."

He is not joking. He is saying: the problem is not that the poor man cannot afford a cow. The problem is that the entire legal and financial system has been rebuilt so that no ordinary man can ever again keep a cow, even if you handed it to him for free.

Then comes the passage everyone quotes but no one understands:

"The whole modern world is looking for a substitute for property… Property is merely the art of democracy. It means that every man should have something that he can shape in his own image, as he is shaped in the image of heaven. But because he is not God, but only a graven image of God, his self-expression must deal with limits; properly with limits that are strict and even small."

Property is democracy, because only when a man owns something real can he say "no" to other men without fear.

Without property he is forced to say "yes" to whoever pays the rent or signs the paycheck.

Next page:

"The man of property… has a little world that is really his own world… He has a little chair that is his chair, a little fire that is his fire, a little cat that is his cat. And when he is tired of them he can cut them up for firewood. But the point is that they are his."

Chesterton is not being sentimental. He is making the coldest political point possible: a civilization that destroys small property destroys the only place where ordinary men practice freedom.

"People will insist that it is impossible for the poor to have property. But it is not impossible for the poor to have property. What is impossible is for the poor to have property while the rich have monopoly."

And one page later, the prophecy that should be carved on the wall of every economics department:

"If we leave things alone, we shall leave everything to the Big Business… and Big Business will leave nothing to anyone at all, not even to his own children."

He wrote that in 1926.

In 2025 the top 1 % owns more wealth than the entire middle class combined. Family farms have almost vanished. The average age of an American farmer is sixty. The phrase "small business" now means "a franchise that pays rent to a corporation."

Chesterton saw it coming because he refused to accept the false choice everyone else accepted: either the state must own everything (socialism) or a few private persons must own everything (monopoly capitalism). He insisted there was a third option: most people owning something.

Then he asked the question no one else dared to ask:

"Why are we more afraid of the small owner than of the large owner?"

His answer is merciless:

"Because the small owner is genuinely independent. He can tell the politician, the advertiser, the tax-collector, even the priest to go to the devil, and still eat. The large owner can only do that by becoming a tyrant himself. Therefore the large owners have always hated the small owners, and have used every law and every tax and every fashion to destroy them."

He ends the chapter with a line that feels written yesterday:

"The world has forgotten that the telephone and the motor-car were invented to serve man. Man has not yet noticed that he is rapidly becoming a servant invented to serve the telephone and the motor-car."

Nine pages that diagnosed 2025 in 1926 with the calm certainty of a physician announcing a terminal illness and then quietly handing the patient the only known cure.

The cure has a name, and Chesterton spends the rest of the book repeating it like a war-cry:

Restore property to the many, or lose freedom for all.

We will let Belloc take the next turn. He is colder, angrier, and even more accurate. And he wrote fourteen years earlier.

Section: 3. The Ten Best Pages of The Servile State (1912)

Put the book in your hands. Turn to Section II ("The Capitalist State Is Unstable") and read through Section IV ("The Servile State"). Ten pages that feel like surgery without anaesthetic.

Belloc begins with a sentence no one in 1912 wanted to hear:

"A society in which the capital is in the hands of a few, while the mass of men are dispossessed of capital and therefore dependent for their livelihood upon the owners of capital, is not a stable society."

He is stating a law of physics.

Then he draws the simplest diagram in political economy:

- If the few keep the capital and the many remain propertyless, the many will eventually revolt.
- The few, being few, cannot win that revolt by open force.
- Therefore the few will offer a bargain: "We will keep our capital, but we will use some of the profit to buy you security (welfare, pensions, health care, minimum wages)."
- The many, being desperate, will accept the bargain.
- The result is not socialism (the many do not own the capital) and not capitalism in the old sense (the few no longer bear the full risk).
- The result is the Servile State: the many are legally free but practically unfree, supported by law yet owned by law.

Belloc published this in 1912.

By 1945 every Western nation had accepted the bargain exactly as he described it. By 2025 the bargain is breaking down (the few have discovered they can keep the capital and cut the security), and the many are again desperate.

Now watch the scalpel go deeper (Section III):

"Under Capitalism the proletarian is free to starve or free to work. Under Collectivism [socialism] he will be compelled to work and compelled not to starve. Under the Servile State he will be compelled to work and legally prevented from starving. The last is the most stable, because it removes the two things men will not endure: starvation and freedom."

Belloc is not celebrating this. He is warning that unless we deliberately choose the distributist alternative (widespread ownership), we will slide into the servile arrangement by default, because it is the only way the owners can stay on top without open civil war.

Then comes the paragraph that should haunt every newsfeed in 2026:

"When capital is universal (that is, concentrated in the hands of a few), and the rest are proletarian, then the State must increasingly intervene to prevent discontent. The wealthy will increasingly use the State to protect their wealth. The poor will increasingly use the State to protect their livelihood. Both will do so at the expense of freedom. The end is a society in which the citizen is secure only when he is obedient."

He wrote that before the income tax had reached 7 %, before social security, before the New Deal, before the NHS, before Amazon's second headquarters subsidy, before universal credit, before corporate bailouts.

And then the final, ice-cold sentence of the book:

"The future of industrial society, left to its own direction, is a Servile State."

Not "might be." Is.

Stand up for a moment and walk to your window. Look at the skyline, the warehouses, the gig drivers, the rented apartments, the closed family farms, the glowing screens that own your attention. That is the Servile State, almost complete.

Belloc saw it coming in 1912 with the same clarity that a man on a hill sees the avalanche before the village hears the rumble.

Chesterton supplied the poetry. Belloc supplied the autopsy.

Together they performed the most astonishing intellectual feat of the twentieth century: they looked at the world everyone said was "progressing" and announced, calmly that it was dying, and they named the only medicine that could still save it.

Next, we will put the two men side by side, note the tiny places they disagreed, and watch how perfectly their agreement outweighs their differences.

Section: 4. Where They Agreed, Where They Differed, Why It Doesn't Matter

Put the two men in the same room and they look like opposites.

Chesterton: vast, laughing, untidy, writing paradoxes at a pub table, beer in one hand, sword-stick in the other. Belloc: lean, fierce, marching twenty miles before breakfast, writing with a cold fury that could slice steel.

Chesterton was primarily a poet who used economics as ammunition. Belloc was primarily a historian who used poetry as a bayonet.

Chesterton wanted England to wake up singing. Belloc wanted England to wake up marching.

Yet when you place the crucial pages side by side, the agreement is overwhelming:

1. Both said the capitalist system is not stable because it rests on a propertyless majority.
2. Both said the socialist "solution" is a mirage that ends in the same concentration of ownership, only painted red.
3. Both said the only real alternative is the widest possible distribution of productive property—farms, workshops, small shops, co-operatives, family firms.
4. Both said the family, not the individual and not the state, is the natural unit of ownership.
5. Both said that once the small owner disappears, freedom disappears with him, no matter how many elections you hold.
6. Both predicted the Servile State—half the population owning everything, half the population dependent on the owners and the state they control.

The differences were real but tactical:

- Chesterton believed the change would begin in the imagination, with stories, songs, and sudden conversions ("England will become distributist the way she became Christian—by a few people going slightly mad with joy").
- Belloc believed it would require laws, land reform, tax policy, and (if necessary) revolution.

- Chesterton was gentler on the old landed aristocracy; Belloc despised them as the original enclosers.
- Chesterton thought the English could be laughed back into sanity; Belloc thought they would have to be frightened into it.

In practice these are temperament differences, not destination differences.

Chesterton supplied the vision you wake up humming. Belloc supplied the map you consult at 3 a.m. when the bailiffs are coming.

Anyone who tries to play them against each other is usually trying to avoid the one thing they both demand: action to restore widespread ownership now.

Imagine a house on fire. One man runs for water and shouts, "Save the children!" The other man runs for water and shouts, "Break the windows so they can breathe!" Only a fool would spend the night arguing about whose plan is more poetic.

The house is still on fire.

The important thing is that both men saw the flames in 1912 and 1926, when almost everyone else smelled only progress.

They saw them, named them, and pointed to the same exit.

We can argue about the exact route later. First let us get out of the building.

Chesterton and Belloc may have written in the shadow of the Great War and Depression, but their diagnosis has not aged. Their central insight, that a healthy society requires the widest possible distribution of productive property, echoes throughout the broader Christian tradition, including voices from the Reformation and its heirs.

The Lutheran economist Wilhelm Röpke extended their critique into a robust "humane economy," grounding it in Reformed ethics, the biblical call to stewardship and vocation, and a fierce defense of small-scale ownership against both monopoly capitalism and collectivism. Similar convictions appear in the Dutch Reformed thinker Abraham Kuyper's doctrine of sphere sovereignty, which insists that the family, the local workshop, and the neighborhood must be protected from being absorbed by either the overweening state or massive corporations. They also resonate with the Southern Agrarians, who defended the household economy and the small farm as bulwarks of liberty and cultural health.

In our own century these ideas continue to find fresh expression among Protestants and other Christians who recognize that true freedom is not abstract but concrete: the ability of ordinary families to own the tools, land, and work that sustain them under Christ the King. Chesterton and Belloc sounded the alarm with poetry and prophecy. Others across the Protestant heritage have carried the torch with theological depth and practical wisdom. The third door remains open, waiting for new hands—whatever their tradition—to push it wider.

Next we will watch their prophecies land, one by one, like artillery shells on the exact coordinates of the year 2025. And we will notice that the one prophecy still hanging in the air is the only one we can still choose to make untrue.

Section: 5. The Prophecies That Came True (and the One That Hasn't Yet)

Here are the predictions they made between 1912 and 1928. Read them in two columns.

What They Said Would Happen	What Actually Happened 1927–2025
Small shops and family farms will be driven out of existence by chain stores and industrial agriculture unless deliberate laws protect them.	In the U.S., 4 corporations now control 85 % of beef processing, 70 % of grocery retail, and 90 % of seed corn. The independent grocer and the family dairy are museum pieces.
The average citizen will own nothing productive and will therefore live in chronic insecurity disguised as "jobs."	In 2024, 60 % of American adults say they could not cover a $1,000 emergency from savings. The median worker has less wealth than the median worker in 1989.
Politicians will promise "security" in exchange for freedom, creating a half-welfare, half-corporate Servile State.	We now have corporate bailouts for the rich, student debt and medical debt for the middle, gig work and food stamps for the bottom, and almost no one in between who can tell the government or the corporation to get lost.
Monopoly capitalism and socialism will gradually merge into one system: private ownership at the top, state compulsion at the bottom.	Amazon receives billions in state subsidies, lobbies for higher minimum wages it can afford and its competitors cannot, and funds political campaigns on both left and right. BlackRock owns stakes in every major company and advises central banks.

What They Said Would Happen	What Actually Happened 1927–2025
The family will disintegrate because it will lack an economic base.	Record profits will coexist with record loneliness and collapsing birth rates.
Culture will become simultaneously glorify consumption and treat ordinary ownership as impossible.	Advertising tells you to "live your best life" while the same companies make it illegal or impossible to repair your own tractor, start a small milk business, or build a house without six permits and a mortgage.

Chesterton (1926): "If the capitalist system continues unchecked, the small man will disappear entirely, and we will be left with a few rich men and a multitude of slaves. The only way to prevent this is the re-creation of widespread property."

Belloc (1912, final paragraph): "The future of industrial society, left to its own direction, is a Servile State… unless men choose, while they are still free to choose, the re-establishment of a Distributive State."

That "unless" is still ringing in the air like a fire bell in the night.

We are not yet fully in the Servile State. The chains are velvet-covered, the contracts are signed with a thumbprint on an app, but the legal possibility of widespread ownership has not been abolished. It has only been forgotten, taxed, zoned, regulated, and ridiculed into the margins.

Everything Chesterton and Belloc wrote leads to a single, non-negotiable conclusion:

If we do nothing, the Servile State arrives in full by 2050 at the latest. If we act, now, while a remnant still remembers what ownership feels like, the household republic is still possible.

They handed us the diagnosis, the warning, and the remedy. All that remains is for us to stop treating their books as museum curiosities and start treating them like the battle plans they actually are.

The next chapter will show you where those plans have already been tried, and quietly succeeded, while the rest of the world was busy watching.

Because history did not end in 1989. It only looked that way for a moment.

Section: 6. A Personal Note from the Author to the Reader

I was twenty-four, with a newborn son at home, working two jobs and pulling sixty to seventy hours a week. There was no gap between sleep and work—just enough time to collapse for a few hours before starting again. I was missing the first months of my boy's life to keep a roof over our heads, and even then I barely had enough money to feed him properly. We lived in a two-bedroom townhouse that always seemed one late paycheck away from eviction. I had nothing to my name, no savings, no family safety net, no degree to fall back on. It was work or go homeless. No third option.

I still believed in capitalism then. I believed in pulling yourself up by your bootstraps. But the boots were worn through and the straps were fraying. I hated the idea of asking for help, especially tax-funded help. I wanted to build something of my own, to stand on my own feet and create a life that actually belonged to us. Yet there was almost no economic room left to take a real risk. The weight of simply surviving felt soul-crushing for a man who just wanted to be a good father.

Many years later, I came across the idea of Distributism. I started with Philip Blond, then found G.K. Chesterton. Together they said what I had felt but couldn't quite name: "You do not have to live like this. There is a door. It is still there. Start pulling."

If you are reading this book, I think you are already feeling the burden of our age.

Maybe you are a young father or mother grinding through endless hours while your children grow up without you. Maybe you are thirty and have never owned anything more permanent than a phone contract. Maybe you are forty and the house you "own" actually owns you. Maybe you are fifty and you look at your grown children and realize they will never afford what you once took for granted. Maybe you are twenty and you just want to know if there is any future in which love, marriage, and children are not economic suicide.

Whoever you are, whatever your politics, these writers have left something for us.

They are not asking you to become a peasant. They are asking you to become free.

The desire for a little place you can call your own, where you and the people you love can live without asking permission every month—is not nostalgia.

The next chapters are going to show you where it is already tied to solid ground, and how to start pulling together.

Chapter 4: A Short History of the Road Not Taken

Section: 1. The Map We Were Never Shown

Every history textbook you ever read in school went roughly like this:

Feudalism → Enclosure → Industrial Revolution → Capitalism vs. Socialism → End of History (choose your winner).

The story was told as if those were the only roads on the map.

There was, in fact, another road. It was wider, better travelled, and far more successful for longer than either of the two we were taught to worship or fear. Millions of ordinary families walked it for centuries. Some are still walking it today.

Yet if you open a standard history of economic thought (Left or Right), you will find little or no mention of:

- the medieval England's open-field villages and guild system
- the Québec habitant farms that fed families for three hundred years
- the Irish Land Acts that turned tenants into owners in one generation
- the fishing villages of Nova Scotia that abolished poverty with study clubs and credit unions
- the Basque valley where 80,000 worker-owners have kept unemployment under 3 % for seventy years

- the 14 million Americans who already own their companies through ESOPs

These are not footnotes. These are countries, provinces, and centuries where the distributist pattern was lived, measured, and proven.

They are simply missing from the curriculum because they embarrass both sides of the official debate.

Capitalist historians skip them because they show that markets work best when ownership is wide, not concentrated. Socialist historians skip them because they show that you can abolish poverty without abolishing private property.

By the time we reach the end, you will know two things with certainty:

1. It has been done before.
2. It is being done now.

And you will never again believe anyone who tells you "there is no alternative."

Section: 2. The Long Memory: Medieval England, Flanders, and Tuscany (1100–1500)

Everyone calls it "feudalism," as if the Middle Ages were one long peasant groan under a mailed fist. The truth is almost the opposite.

For roughly four centuries, most of Western Europe lived in the closest thing to a distributist civilization the world has ever seen at scale.

Take a single year—say 1300—and walk through three ordinary landscapes.

First, an English Midland village. Ninety percent of the land is worked in open fields divided into thousands of narrow strips. Every villager (free or villein) holds thirty to sixty scattered strips, enough to feed a family and produce a small surplus. The commons supply grazing, firewood, nuts, berries, thatch. The lord's demesne is worked partly by labor service, but even more by hired free labor paid in coin or grain. The village court, run by the peasants themselves, decides cropping and grazing rules. Guilds in the nearby town guarantee that a journeyman baker or blacksmith can become his own master in seven years. No one is rich; almost no one is propertyless.

And here is the detail that makes modern jaws drop: the typical peasant worked roughly 160–180 days a year on the lord's demesne or his own strips. The rest of the year belonged to family, church, festival, and what we would now call "leisure." Historian Christopher Dyer, surveying manorial accounts, found that after obligatory labor and Sundays were subtracted, the medieval villager had more holidays than a modern French civil servant. As Juliet Schor titled her famous study, they were "The Overworked American's" ancestors only in the sense that they knew how to stop working.

Second, the polders of Flanders. Free peasant families own small, intensely cultivated farms reclaimed from the sea by dykes they built and maintain together. Towns like Bruges and Ghent are governed by craft guilds; a master weaver owns his loom, his house, and usually a vineyard outside the walls. When a plague or war kills a third of the population in 1348–50, the survivors simply inherit more strips and tools. Wages soar, serfdom vanishes, and the standard of living for ordinary craftsmen is higher than it will be again until the 1950s.

Third, the hills of Tuscany. The contadini (sharecroppers) work under the famous mazedia contract: the landlord supplies the farmstead and half the seed; the peasant family supplies labor and the other half. At harvest the crop is divided 50/50. The peasant family lives in its own stone house, keeps chickens, pigs, olive trees, and a vineyard rows. The contract is hereditary; evictions are almost unheard of. When the Black Death strikes, the surviving families negotiate better terms and many become outright owners within two generations.

In all three places the pattern is the same:

- Productive assets (land, tools, workshops) are owned or securely held by the families, not by absentee investors.
- Large estates exist, but they cannot swallow the small without breaking customary or canon law.
- Guilds and village courts protect the little man against the big.
- The Church teaches (and largely enforces) the "just price" and the prohibition on usury, keeping credit cooperative rather than predatory.
- Population is high, but famines are regional and rare; life expectancy for those who reach adulthood is close to modern levels.

As historian Reginald Gretton wrote in The Myth of Feudalism (still the best short demolition of the Dickensian caricature):

"The idea that the medieval peasant was a downtrodden slave who toiled from dawn to dusk every day of his life is one of the most persistent myths of popular history… In reality he enjoyed an amount of leisure that the modern factory worker or salaried employee would find unbelievable."

He enjoyed that leisure because he was, to a significant degree, his own master.

He was not rich, but he was not a proletarian.

He owned, or securely held, the tools of his livelihood.

That single fact bought him time—time for children, for prayer, for brewing ale, for dancing around the Maypole, for simply sitting in the sun.

This was not paradise. War, plague, and occasional brutal lords existed. But for the average family the economic position was dramatically more secure than that of an Amazon warehouse worker or a Uber driver in 2025.

The proof is in the demographics: Europe's population doubled between 1000 and 1300, something that only happens when ordinary people have enough food, hope, and freedom to marry young and raise children.

Then the enclosures, the statism of the religious wars, and the rise of commercial capitalism began to dismantle it.

But it lasted four hundred years and supported tens of millions.

It was not a dream.

And every time it has been tried again, in smaller patches, it has worked again.

The long memory is still alive. The next places kept the flame burning quietly for centuries after the official histories declared it extinct.

Section: 3. The Catholic Countryside That Refused to Die

While the rest of Europe was busy turning peasants into proletarians, a few corners of the Catholic world simply refused to go along.

Québec, 1600–1950 When the English conquered New France in 1759, they expected the French-speaking habitants to disappear within a generation. Instead, the habitant farm system (long, narrow riverfront lots stretching back from the St Lawrence) proved indestructible. Each son received his own strip when he married; the family cleared forest together, built in stone, and paid almost no rent to absentee landlords. By 1900 Québec had the highest birth rate in the Western world (over 7 children per woman in some parishes) and almost no urban proletariat. Priests preached Rerum Novarum from the pulpit; credit unions (caisses populaires) founded by Alphonse Desjardins in 1900 spread like wildfire. Even in the 1940s, two-thirds of Quebecers still lived on family-owned land or in small towns where the majority were self-employed. The industrial revolution arrived late and gently, because the people already owned enough to say "non, merci."

Rural Ireland before the Famine (and in the West after) The classic picture of pre-Famine Ireland is one of misery. The classic picture is wrong. In the west and south, the rundale system (joint families farming scattered strips with common grazing) kept the majority of households in possession of land and cattle. Travelers in the 1830s were stunned by the size and cheerfulness of the cabins, the abundance of milk, butter, and potatoes, and the fact that "the Irish peasant works only when he feels like it." When the Famine struck, the real killer was not overpopulation; it was the prior concentration of land in the hands of absentee

Protestant landlords. In the post-Famine West, where Gaelic culture and the old clan memory survived, families clung to their small holdings with fanatic tenacity. By 1900–1950, while the rest of Europe emptied its villages, the west of Ireland kept its people on the land, speaking Irish, dancing at the crossroads, and producing large families on farms that were tiny by American standards but sufficient by any human standard.

The Tyrol (Austria/Italy) High in the Alps, the inheritance law was simple: the farm passes undivided to one child, but the others receive cash portions and the lifelong right to live and work on the land. Result: almost every mountain valley is still dotted with family-owned farms and small workshops. In 2024 the region has one of the lowest unemployment rates of youth emigration in Europe, near-zero rural poverty, and a birth rate well above the Italian average. The local saying is "We don't have jobs; we have homes that give us work."

Central Italy – the mazedia heartland Even after the mazedia sharecropping contracts were abolished in the 1960s, the culture they created did not die. Families who had worked the same hills for five centuries simply bought the land when it came on the market. Today the provinces of Tuscany and Emilia-Romagna have the highest density of small family farms and artisan businesses in Europe, the highest life expectancy, and the highest percentage of young adults who still live within ten kilometers of their parents. The co-ops that grew out of the old mazedia spirit (Parmesan, Parma ham, balsamic vinegar) are global brands, yet the profits still circulate in the same villages.

What all these places had in common:

- Strong Christian culture that treated the family farm as sacred

- Legal systems that made it hard to accumulate huge estates
- Credit systems (caisses populaires, Raiffeisen banks, parish funds) that served households, not speculators
- A stubborn refusal to trade inheritance for "progress"

They were not museum exhibits. They were living, fertile, singing proof that the medieval pattern could survive gunpowder, Napoleon, and the railway.

The industrial world laughed at them and predicted their disappearance by 1950. They are still here. Their children still speak the old dialects, still keep the old feasts, and still own the old land.

The old land owns them back.

These were the quiet rearguard actions. The next section will show the frontal assaults (places where people in the twentieth century deliberately chose the distributist road and won stunning victories in a single generation.

The flame went underground, but it never went out. Sometimes it flared up so brightly that even the modern world had to blink.

Section: 4. The 19th-Century Fight-Back

While the industrial world was busy declaring the small owner extinct, ordinary people in several countries simply refused to die.

They fought back with laws, loans, and sheer stubbornness—and they won.

Ireland: The Land War and the Greatest Peaceful Redistribution in History 1845–1909 After the Famine, British landlords owned 95 % of Ireland and rented it to tenants who could be evicted on a whim. Between 1879 and 1909 a peasant movement (the Land League, led by Michael Davitt and backed by Parnell and the Church) combined rent strikes, boycotts, and political pressure until Parliament passed a series of Land Purchase Acts. The mechanism was brilliantly distributist: the government lent tenants the money to buy their farms at fair prices; the loan was repaid over 68 years at 3.25 % interest out of the former rent. Result: by 1920 more than 70 % of Irish farmers owned their land outright—the largest peaceful transfer of property from large estates to small family owners in modern history. In the West of Ireland today you can still see the stone walls and whitewashed cottages built by those new owners. Their grandchildren are still farming the same fields.

Germany and Austria: The Raiffeisen Revolution 1850s–1900 Friedrich Wilhelm Raiffeisen, a Catholic mayor in the Rhineland, watched starving peasants borrow from moneylenders at 50–100 % interest. His answer: village credit cooperatives owned by the members themselves. You put in one mark, you get one vote. Profits stay in the village and are lent only to members for productive purposes—buying a cow, a plough, seed. By 1914 there were 17,000 Raiffeisen banks with 4 million members. Today the Raiffeisen group is the largest private employer in Austria and still refuses to lend for speculation. The small family farm in Bavaria and the Tyrol survived the 20th century largely because Raiffeisen kept the moneylenders out.

Denmark: The Folk High School Miracle 1860s–1900 While the Prussian army was crushing Danish armies, a Lutheran bishop named N.F.S. Grundtvig started “schools for life” where young farmers spent winters studying history, poetry, and cooperative economics instead of Latin and Greek. The graduates went home and turned bankrupt estates into cooperative creameries, bacon factories, and purchasing associations. By 1914 Denmark—poor, rocky, defeated in war—had become the richest agricultural nation per capita in Europe. 90 % of its butter was produced by farmer-owned co-ops. The Danish countryside still runs on the same model: one in three Danes is a member of a cooperative, and the birth rate in rural areas remains above replacement.

Three different countries, three different religions (Catholic Ireland, Catholic-Lutheran Germany, Lutheran Denmark), one identical recipe:

1. Secure the family in possession of productive assets (land, cows, tools).
2. Give them cheap, patient, member-owned credit.
3. Teach them that small is not pathetic; small is powerful when linked together.

No central planning. No billionaires. No gulags.

Just millions of new owners who refused to become proletarians.

The 19th century said the peasant was doomed. The peasants answered with ballots, credit unions, and butter.

They won.

The 20th century would produce victories that were louder, faster, and even more astonishing.

Next stop: a priest-led fishing villages in Nova Scotia that abolished poverty in fifteen years, and a Basque village that built an industrial empire owned by its workers while Franco's tanks were still rolling.

Section: 5. The 20th-Century Miracles

Now the flame bursts into open daylight. Three places, three decades apart, three different languages, one identical result: when ordinary people deliberately set out to make every family an owner, poverty collapses, wages rise, and the culture comes back to life.

1. Antigonish Movement – Nova Scotia, 1920s–1950s British-owned coal and steel companies paid Cape Breton miners in scrip and kept fishermen in perpetual debt to company stores. Two priests at St Francis Xavier University (Father Jimmy Tompkins and Father Moses Coady) decided to try the one thing no government or corporation had ever tried: teach the workers how to own). They started "study clubs" in kitchens and parish halls. Ten fishermen or miners would meet once a week, read Rerum Novarum, study bookkeeping, and ask one question: "Why are we poor in debt when we produce everything?" Within fifteen years they had built:

- 142 credit unions
- 47 cooperative lobster canneries
- adult-education schools in every parish
- housing co-ops that built entire streets of worker-owned homes

By 1950 the region had gone from the poorest in Canada to full employment and the highest home-ownership rate in the province. Poverty did not "decline." It disappeared. Father Coady's famous line was: "The Kings of England could not do it. The Rockefellers could not do it. But we did it with study clubs and kitchen meetings."

2. Mondragón – Basque Country, 1956–today Franco's dictatorship had crushed Basque culture and condemned the town of Arrasate-Mondragón to unemployment. A young priest named José María Arizmendiarrieta arrived in 1941 with nothing but a battered copy of Quadragesimo Anno. He started a technical school. In 1956 five of his graduates opened a small paraffin-heater workshop with £30,000 scraped together from neighbors. Today the Mondragón Cooperative Corporation is the seventh-largest business group in Spain:

- 80,000 worker-owners
- €12 billion annual revenue
- supermarkets, banks, factories, a university, the world's largest worker-co-op research centre
- top salary never more than 9× the lowest (usually 5–6×)
- unemployment rate in the valley: under 3 % even during Spain's worst recessions
- almost zero permanent layoffs (workers are moved to other co-ops instead)

When outsiders ask, "How do you compete with Chinese wages?" the answer is always the same: "We own the machines. They don't."

3. Emilia-Romagna – Northern Italy, 1945–today After the Second World War the "Red Belt" of Italy (communist-voting, fiercely Catholic) decided to reject both Moscow and Milan. They copied the old mazedia spirit into modern law: generous tax breaks and cheap credit for worker cooperatives. Result: one-third of the region's GDP now comes from co-ops. Bologna has more cooperative businesses per capita than anywhere else on

earth. Parma ham, Parmesan cheese, balsamic vinegar, Ferrari, Lamborghini—many of the brands you think are "corporate" are actually produced by networks of small and medium co-ops. Per-capita income is 50 % above the Italian average, unemployment half the national rate, and the birth rate the highest in Italy.

Three miracles, three lessons:

- Antigonish shows you can start with almost nothing if you start with education and credit unions.
- Mondragón shows you can build heavy industry and high technology on worker ownership and still beat the multinationals.
- Emilia-Romagna shows you can do it at regional scale under modern conditions and still keep the streets full of children.

No billionaires were required. No five-year plans were required. Only one thing was required: the deliberate decision to make the worker the owner.

These are not tiny experiments. Together they involve tens of millions of people and trillions of dollars of assets.

And they are still growing.

The 20th century told us distributism was impossible. The 20th century lied.

Next we will cross the Atlantic and discover that the quietest revolution of all has been happening in the United States for fifty years—while almost no one was looking.

Section: 6. The American Experiments Nobody Talks About

America loves to tell itself it invented free enterprise, yet it has quietly carried out the largest distributist experiment on earth, almost entirely under the radar of both Left and Right.

Employee Stock Ownership Plans (ESOPs) 1974–today In 1974 a Louisiana economist and senator named Russell Long slipped a few paragraphs into the tax code that allowed companies to sell shares to their workers on favorable terms. Almost nobody noticed.

Today:

- 6,500 companies are 100 % or majority employee-owned through ESOPs
- 14 million American workers are direct owners of their firms (more than the entire membership of U.S. labor unions)
- $1.9 trillion in assets are held in ESOP accounts
- the average employee-owner has roughly $134,000 in company stock on top of their wages
- ESOP companies grow 2.5 % faster per year, lay off workers at one-third the rate of conventional firms, and have retirement accounts 3–5 times larger

Names you know, but never knew were worker-owned: Publix Super Markets (230,000 worker-owners), WinCo Foods, Bob's Red Mill, Hy-Vee grocery chain, and thousands of smaller manufacturers, construction firms, and engineering companies.

Most of these firms are boringly profitable, boringly stable, and boringly invisible to the financial press, because they are not trying to make a few venture capitalists rich. They are trying to make ordinary families independent.

The Catholic Rural-Life Movement and the Back-to-the-Land Surge 1920s–1950s While the New Deal was busy worshipping bigness, Catholic bishops, priests, and laymen launched a counter-revolution: the National Catholic Rural Life Conference (founded 1923). They bought abandoned farms, taught soil conservation and cooperative marketing, and resettled thousands of urban families on small holdings. In the Upper Midwest and the movement created entire counties where the majority of residents were still owner-operator farmers into the 1960s. Their newsletter proudly reprinted Chesterton and Belloc; their motto was "The Land for the Man, Not the Man for the Land."

The Southern Agrarians 1930 Twelve Vanderbilt University poets and professors published *I'll Take My Stand*, a fiery defense of the small farm, the family business, and the "human scale" against the "industrial gospel." Dismissed at the time as nostalgic, the book has been continuously in print ever since. Its economic chapters read like a blueprint for everything that later worked in Antigonish, Mondragón, and ESOPs.

The Grange and the Farm Bureau cooperatives 1867–present American farmers, refusing to be crushed by railroads and banks, built their own grain elevators, creameries, and supply co-ops. At their peak in the 1930s, farmer co-ops handled 30 % of all U.S. agricultural marketing. Many are still alive (Land O'Lakes, Ocean Spray, Sunkist), quietly distributing billions in profits back to member-families instead of to Wall Street.

Add it all together and you discover something astonishing:

Roughly one in eight working-age Americans already participates in some form of distributist structure (ESOPs, co-ops, family farms, credit unions). They simply never learned the word for what they are doing.

The American experiment is not a footnote. It is the largest ongoing distributist reality in the world, hidden in plain sight because it refuses to wear an ideology.

And it works.

ESOP workers retire with ten times the wealth of their peers. Co-op regions show higher life satisfaction and lower divorce rates. Family-farm counties still have the highest birth rates in the country.

The road not taken? America has been walking it for fifty years. We just forgot to put up the sign.

Next we will look at places that are still planting new signs today, in Taiwan, Kerala, Alaska, and even in the middle of American cities where tenants are buying their apartment buildings out from under the hedge funds.

Section: 7. The Places That Are Doing It Right Now

You do not need to wait for a new pope, a new president, or a new revolution. People are widening ownership today, on every continent, under every kind of government.

Taiwan – The Small-Firm Miracle 99.8 % of Taiwanese businesses have fewer than 200 employees. The average firm has six workers. Yet Taiwan is one of the twenty richest economies on earth, with a Gini coefficient (inequality measure) lower than Sweden's. How? Family-owned factories pass from parents to children, government credit favors small borrowers, and export networks are built on trust, not venture capital. Result: the highest density of millionaires-per-capita who still show up to work in polo shirts and flip-flops.

Kerala, India – The Cooperative State One-third of the population belongs to a cooperative. Hospitals, banks, schools, coconut processing, even the famous Kudumbashree women's micro-enterprise network (4.5 million members) are owned by the people who use them. Kerala has India's highest literacy, longest life expectancy, and lowest infant mortality—on an income per capita one-tenth the U.S. level. The secret: ownership instead of handouts.

Alaska Permanent Fund Dividend Since 1982 every Alaskan resident (man, woman, child) receives an annual cheque from the state's oil wealth—typically $1,000–$2,000 per year, no strings attached. It is not welfare; it is a citizen's dividend from commonly owned resources. Result: the most equal state in the U.S., the lowest poverty rate in America for children, and a political consensus that lasts across parties.

Japan's Neighborhood Factories Walk through the Ōta ward in Tokyo or the Higashi-Osaka district: thousands of small and medium factories, each 10–80 workers, family-owned for generations, making precision parts for Toyota, Sony, Boeing. They pay middle-class wages, almost never lay off, and still dominate global markets in niches too small for multinational giants. The phrase "lifetime employment" survives here because the workers are often literal cousins of the owner.

U.S. Cities – Tenants Buying the Building In New York, Washington D.C., and Oakland, limited-equity housing cooperatives and community land trusts are quietly purchasing apartment buildings from hedge funds. Once bought, rents are capped forever, and every resident becomes a voting member-owner. In 2025 over 500,000 Americans already live in such buildings, and the pipeline is growing by 10–15 % a year. BlackRock can outbid them on price, but it cannot outbid them on patience.

A few more flashes:

- Evergreen Cooperatives in Cleveland: worker-owned solar, laundry, and greenhouse businesses employing ex-prisoners in the city's poorest neighborhoods.
- The Scottish island of Eigg: residents bought their island from an absentee landlord in 1997 and now run wind, hydro, and tourism for themselves.
- Preston, England: the local council redirected £ billions of public spending into worker co-ops; unemployment fell 20 % in five years.

None of these places is perfect. All of them are growing.

What they share is a deliberate choice: instead of waiting for the market or the state to save them, ordinary people decided to own the things that matter—land, houses, machines, energy, food—and to own them together in forms that cannot be sold out from under their children.

They are not waiting for permission. They are simply doing it.

And every year the list gets longer.

The road not taken is now a six-lane highway. You just have to know where to look.

Next, one page to tie it all together: the pattern that appears every single time the experiment is run. You will recognize it instantly, because it is the pattern written into Genesis, into the Gospels, and into your own heart.

Section: 8. The Pattern That Always Wins

Look at every place we have visited (medieval England, Québec, Ireland after the Land Acts, Antigonish, Mondragón, Emilia-Romagna, the ESOP heartland of the American Midwest, Taiwan, Kerala, Alaska) and five elements appear every single time, as predictable as sunrise:

1. Productive property is in the hands of the many, not the few. (Land, tools, machines, equity, or a permanent dividend—something that earns while you sleep.)
2. The family household (not the lone individual and not the state) is treated as the normal economic unit. Laws, taxes, and credit are tilted toward the married couple with children.
3. Finance serves production, not speculation. Credit unions, Raiffeisen banks, patient capital, zero-interest parish loans, ESOP leverage—money is a servant, never the master.
4. Subsidiarity is real: decisions and ownership stay as close to the kitchen table as possible. No distant bureaucracy or distant shareholder can overrule the people who actually do the work and live with the consequences.
5. The culture celebrates the small owner instead of mocking him. The successful farmer, the master craftsman, the worker who retires a millionaire because he owns shares in his own factory—these are the heroes, not the quirky exceptions.

When these five conditions are present, the same results follow with the boring reliability of a law of nature:

- Poverty collapses
- Inequality shrinks without coercion

- Birth rates rise
- Crime falls
- People stay put instead of fleeing to cities
- Work feels like stewardship instead of servitude
- The Sabbath becomes possible again

When even one of the five is missing, the experiment weakens or dies.

This is not theory. It is history's largest and longest empirical test.

The medieval village had all five. Mondragón has all five. The Irish small farmer after 1909 had all five. The Amazon warehouse worker in 2025 has none.

That is the entire difference between a human life and a proletarian existence.

Everything we have seen in this chapter (centuries, continents, religions, technologies) is simply the same five-note melody played on different instruments.

The melody has never failed when it was played faithfully.

It is still being played today in more places than ever before.

And the sheet music is lying on the table in front of you.

These are not footnotes. These are proof.

The road not taken was never closed. It was only hidden.

Now you have the map.

The rest of the book is about how to start walking.

Chapter 5: Capitalism's Children

Section: 1. The Promise and the Bait-and-Switch

When capitalism was young and still had to sell itself to a world of kings and peasants, it made one very specific promise.

It went something like this:

"Break up the old monopolies of land and guild. Let anyone buy and sell freely. Let the clever and the hardworking rise. In time, capital will spread downward and outward. Factories, shops, and farms will multiply. Wages will rise. Savings will grow. Every diligent man will own their own homes, their own businesses, their own futures. The children of servants will become masters in their turn.

That was the pitch in 1776, in 1848, in 1890, in 1945. It was printed on recruitment posters for the New World, preached from Methodist pulpits, sung in Horatio Alger novels, and repeated by every politician who ever waved the flag of free enterprise.

It was a good promise. It sounded like common sense. It sounded like justice.

Here is what actually happened instead.

The monopolies were broken, all right. But they were broken the way ice is broken on a river: the fragments floated downstream and froze together again into bigger sheets. Only now the monopolies were no longer bound by tradition, religion, or royal charter. They were bound by nothing except the legal right to grow without limit.

Land became an investment class. Tools became corporate assets. Knowledge became intellectual property. Even human attention became inventory.

The clever and hardworking did rise. A few of them rose so high they could buy the entire ladder and pull it up after them.

The rest discovered that the promise had quietly changed.

No one announced the change. There was no press conference. The fine print simply shifted, year by year, until the promise now reads:

"Let the market work and a tiny minority will own almost everything. The rest of you will rent your lives back from them in the form of wages, subscriptions, licenses, and debt. You will call this freedom because you can choose which brand of chain you wear."

The original promise has not been broken. It has been bought out.

In 1950 the typical American family needed one income to buy a house, raise four children, save for retirement, and take a two-week vacation every summer. In 2025 the typical American family needs two full-time incomes, side hustles, and still cannot afford the house their grandparents bought on one salary.

That is not a glitch. That is the feature.

Capitalism kept its word to someone. It just wasn't to you.

The next pages will show exactly how thoroughly the promise was kept to the top 0.1 %, and exactly how completely it was broken for everyone else.

We will look at the numbers without hysteria, the way a doctor shows you an X-ray and says, "This is what the bone actually looks like now."

Because once you see the fracture clearly, you stop calling it "prosperity."

Section: 2. The Vanishing Middle: Wealth Concentration in Real Time

Let us look at the X-ray.

Year	**989**	**024**
Top 10 % share of total U.S. wealth	7 %	6 %
Top 1 % share	3 %	5 %
Top 0.1 % share	%	5 %
Bottom 50 % share	.7 %	.5 %
Corporate stock owned by bottom 50 %	4 %	1 %

Three individuals (Elon Musk, Jeff Bezos, Mark Zuckerberg on any given day) now possess more wealth than the entire bottom half of the United States—165 million people.

Corporate profits as a percentage of GDP are at the highest level since 1945. Median real wages (adjusted for inflation) are roughly where they were in 1979.

In 1980 the CEO of a typical large company earned about 42 times the average worker. In 2024 the ratio is 344 times—and that is only the reported salary; total compensation including stock awards is often 1,000 times or more.

The most telling chart is the one nobody puts on television:

Wealth of a typical American family headed by someone with a high-school diploma 1950 → 2025 (inflation-adjusted)

- 1950: could buy a house, a car, raise four children on one income
- 2025: cannot buy a house, cannot save for retirement, cannot survive a single missed paycheck

The same story repeats in every developed country that embraced the pure market model.

Housing tells the story most brutally. In 1970 the median U.S. home cost 2.9 times the median household income. In 2025 it costs 8.2 times, after interest rates briefly spiked, the ratio is now closer to 9 times in many cities. In Greater London, Sydney, Toronto, Vancouver, Auckland the ratio is 12–15 times.

The result is not mysterious:

- Record corporate profits
- Record stock-market highs
- Record number of billionaires
- Record number of working homeless
- Record levels of household debt
- Record low fertility among people under forty

The middle is not shrinking because people suddenly became lazy. The middle is shrinking because the ownership of productive assets has been vacuumed upward at a speed never seen before in human history.

BlackRock, Vanguard, and State Street together vote roughly 25 % of shares in every S&P 500 company. Amazon controls 50 % of U.S. online retail and is on track for 70 %. Four companies slaughter 85 % of American beef. Two companies control 90 % of the global smartphone operating-system market.

This is not the "free market" anyone promised in 1776 or 1890 or 1945. This is oligarchy wearing the mask of competition.

The promise was dispersal of capital. The result was the most successful concentration of capital the world has ever seen.

And the concentration is still accelerating.

If you are under forty and do not come from wealth, the numbers say calmly, mathematically—that the game is no longer rigged.

Next we will walk through the house of an ordinary family in 2025 and watch, room by room, how the fracture touches every part of their life.

Section: 3. The Family Under the Algorithm

Come inside the house.

It is 6:47 p.m. on a Thursday in 2025. The lights are on, the Wi-Fi is strong, and the monthly budget is already $412 in the red.

Living room Both parents are still at work. Dad is driving for a rideshare app because the warehouse cut overtime. Mom is finishing charts for a client #3 because her full-time salary no longer covers daycare. The eight-year-old is watching YouTube on a tablet that costs $29 a month to rent-to-own. The five-year-old is asleep on the couch because the second bedroom became a home office when rent went up 22 % in two years.

Kitchen The refrigerator is stocked, but only because they used the credit card with the 29.9 % interest rate. Groceries now take 18 % of take-home pay (it was 9 % in 1980). The parents joke that ramen is the new steak; they are only half joking.

Bedroom The mortgage (or rent) payment is 48 % of net income. In 1970 it was 21 %. They will be paying it until they are seventy-two, assuming interest rates ever come down again. The house has doubled in nominal price since they bought it eight years ago, but their equity is still negative because they needed a low-down-payment loan at 7.25 %.

Bathroom cabinet Prescriptions for the kids' ear infections sit unfilled because the deductible reset in January. Total medical debt: $18,000 and growing.

Garage (or parking lot) Two cars, both leased, because buying outright was impossible and repairs on anything older than five years cost more than the car is worth. Car insurance is $340 a month.

Phones Four lines, $240 a month, non-negotiable, because both jobs require constant availability and the kids' school apps only work on smartphones.

The monthly budget looks like this:

Category	1980 (one income)	2025 (two incomes + side hustles)
Housing	21 %	48 %
Transportation	12 %	19 %
Food	14 %	18 %
Health care	6 %	14 %
Education/debt service	2 %	16 %

Category	1980 (one income)	2025 (two incomes + side hustles)
Everything else	45 %	−15 % (deficit)

They are not wasteful. They are not stupid. They are the statistical median family.

Now the human numbers that no spreadsheet catches:

- They have not had a week-long vacation in six years.
- They have not had a full weekend together in four months.
- They have not made love in the daylight since the youngest was born, because someone is always exhausted or on a shift.
- They have stopped talking about a third child because the numbers literally will not allow it.

Fertility collapse is not a cultural mystery. It is an economic equation.

Across the developed world, the total fertility rate now sits between 0.9 (South Korea) and 1.8 (France). Every single study that controls for housing-cost-to-income ratio finds the same brutal correlation: when shelter costs exceed roughly 30 % of income, people stop having children. When it exceeds 45 %, they stop almost stop entirely.

Capitalism promised that markets would make children affordable by making everything cheaper. Instead it made children unaffordable by making everything that matters—land, houses, education, medical care, into speculative assets.

The algorithm does not hate families. It simply has no column for them.

It counts eyeballs, clicks, deliveries, and quarterly returns. A married couple raising four children on one modest income is an error message.

The family has become what G.K. Chesterton predicted in 1926: "too expensive for the poor."

That is not a side effect. That is the entire business model.

Next we will walk outside the house and meet the new digital serfs who do not even pretend to own anything—not the car they drive, not the phone they use, not the code that decides whether they eat tomorrow.

The enclosure of the commons has moved online. The peasants are still being cleared. Only now the clearing happens with a software update at 3 a.m. and a polite email that says "Your account has been deactivated."

Section: 4. The New Digital Feudalism

Step outside the mortgaged house and meet the people who no longer even have a house to lose.

They are the fastest-growing workforce in the developed world: the gig proletariat.

- The Uber driver who logs 70 hours a week but owns neither the car (leased) nor the algorithm that sends him to the airport at 2 a.m.
- The DoorDash courier on a bicycle paid $3.19 per delivery after expenses.
- The Amazon Flex driver who must scan a QR code every 90 minutes to prove he has not stopped for a bathroom break.

- The content moderator in Manila or Nairobi who is paid $2 an hour to watch beheadings so your social feed stays "safe."
- The TaskRabbit handyman who is rated, ranked, and deactivated by strangers with one click.

None of them own the platform. None of them can pass the "job" to their children. All of them can be turned off like a light switch.

This is not a bug. It is the logical endpoint of the ownership vacuum.

Medieval villeins at least owned their own hoe, their own farm animals, and the strips they worked. They owed labor service, but the lord could not suddenly move their cottage to another county or change the rules overnight. The modern gig worker owns nothing except his smartphone (which he is still paying off) and can be evicted from the platform with less ceremony than a 14th-century lord needed to evict a serf.

The language has changed, but the structure is eerily familiar:

Medieval Serf (1300)	**Digital Serf (2025)**
Tied to the manor	Tied to the app
Paid in kind or small coin	Paid per task, no benefits
Could not leave without permission	Deactivated without appeal
Lord took a percentage of harvest	Platform takes 20–40 % of every fare
Tools supplied by lord	Car/phone supplied by

Medieval Serf (1300)	Digital Serf (2025)
	worker
Security: could not starve	Insecurity: can be cut off tomorrow

The medieval serf had one advantage: the Church and custom limited how much the lord could squeeze. The digital serf has no such protection. When Uber drops the per-mile rate by 25 % overnight, there is no village court to cry foul. There is only the "independent contractor agreement" you clicked without reading.

The numbers are no longer estimates; they are official:

- 36 % of the U.S. workforce now does some form of gig or contingent work
- 59 million Americans performed platform work in the last year
- Median annual earnings for full-time Uber drivers (after expenses): ≈ $38,000 in large cities, less than a starting warehouse job with benefits
- 78 % of gig workers live paycheck to paycheck (vs. 47 % of traditional employees)

And the concentration is even more extreme than in traditional industries:

- Two apps (Uber and Lyft) control 98 % of the U.S. ride-hail market
- One company (Amazon) controls 70 % of U.S. e-book sales, 50 % of online retail, and 90 % of the cloud server market that powers most start-ups
- Four platforms (Facebook, Instagram, Google, TikTok) harvest 95 % of global digital advertising revenue

The feudal lord has been replaced by the algorithm. The castle has been replaced by a data center in Oregon cooled by your electricity bill. The peasants still till the fields; only now the fields are invisible, and the harvest is attention, location, and purchasing history.

This is not the temporary awkward phase of a new technology. This is the mature form of unchecked capital: a world where almost everything that produces wealth is owned by a handful of funds and platforms, and almost everyone else is reduced to renting their own time by the minute.

The medieval peasant at least went home to a cottage he could not be evicted from. The digital peasant goes home to an apartment he can be priced out of the moment the algorithm decides to raise the rent.

They call it "disruption." They used to call it "enclosure."

Same road, faster car.

Next we will step back inside the soul of the family and look at the wound that no amount of money can ever heal. Because the deepest damage is not done to the bank account. It is done to the human heart.

Section: 5. The Spiritual Wound

The money wound is obvious. The spiritual wound is quieter, but it bleeds longer.

It is the wound of a man who wakes at 4:30 a.m. to drive a truck he does not own, for a company he will never meet, on roads he will never control, knowing that his son is learning to read from a screen because Dad is never home at bedtime.

It is the wound of a woman who once dreamed of teaching her daughters to bake bread, but now teaches them to scan QR codes for dinner because she is on her second shift and the daycare closes at six sharp.

It is the wound of children who grow up believing that "work" means staring at a glowing rectangle until your eyes burn, and that "success" means being allowed to stare at a slightly larger rectangle in a slightly nicer room.

Capitalism did not merely take away the three acres and the cow. It took away the very possibility of a vocation.

In a distributist order a man's work is tied to a place, a craft, a family, a future. He sharpens tools that will belong to his son. He improves land that will feed his grandchildren. He can say, with the full weight of reality behind the words, "This is mine, and I am making it better."

In the capitalist order most work is abstract, interchangeable, and owned by strangers. The warehouse picker does not know where the box will end up. The coder does not meet the user. The Uber driver does not own the route. The product of their labor disappears into a supply chain whose final beneficiary they will never see.

The result is not just insecurity. It is meaninglessness disguised as employment.

You can measure the wound in the suicide statistics: Prime-age men (25–54) in the United States now kill themselves at three times the rate they did in 1950. The sharpest rises are in rural counties that lost their farms and factory towns that lost their factories.

You can measure it in the quiet despair of "quiet quitting," in the explosion of anxiety medication, in the fact that the most common sentence young adults now say about the future is "I can't imagine bringing children into this."

You can measure it in the collapse of the Sabbath. When both parents must work flat out simply to pay for shelter, there is no seventh day. There is only the next shift, the next gig, the next payment plan. The commandment to rest becomes a luxury good available only to the top decile.

The spiritual wound has a precise location: the place where inheritance used to live.

In every healthy civilization, a young couple could confidently expect to receive (by gift, by savings, by clearing the back forty) enough productive property to start their own household. Today the same young couple starts adult life with negative net worth and the knowledge that almost nothing they earn will ever truly belong to them.

They are not citizens of a commonwealth. They are tenants of an algorithm.

Chesterton saw this coming in 1926:

"The tragedy of the poor is that they can no longer own property. The tragedy of the rich is that they can no longer imagine why anyone would want to."

The rich have won the argument so completely that most of us have forgotten there ever was an alternative.

We treat the wound the way peasants once treated plague: we call it normal, we medicate it with Netflix and SSRIs, and we tell the children to be grateful they are not starving.

But the soul knows the difference between a wage and a birthright.

And the soul is dying of the difference.

When we arrive at the next chapter we will watch the same soul-killing pattern appear under the other great modern experiment (socialism), only wearing a different uniform and speaking with a different accent.

Because the wound is not left-wing or right-wing. It is the wound of a world that has forgotten the human scale.

And it bleeds the same color no matter who holds the knife.

Section: 6. The Myth of the Meritocracy

We are told one last comforting story to keep the wound from hurting too much:

"If you are smart and work hard, you can still make it. The ladder is still there. It's just taller."

That story is now provably false.

- Sixty percent of American household wealth is inherited, not earned.
- A child born into the top 1 % of income has a 50 % chance of staying in the top 10 % as an adult. A child born into the bottom 10 % has a 4 % chance of reaching the top 10 %.
- Ivy League universities now admit more students from the top 1 % of income than from the entire bottom 50 %.
- The correlation between parental wealth and SAT scores is now higher than the correlation between SAT scores and college admission.

The Horatio Alger hero (poor boy works hard, becomes millionaire) is statistically rarer than a person struck by lightning twice.

Even the lightning-strike winners know the game is fixed. Listen to them when they forget the microphone is on:

Nick Hanauer, billionaire venture capitalist, 2014: "The pitchforks are coming… If we don't do something to fix the glaring inequities in this economy, the pitchforks are going to come for us."

Warren Buffett, 2011: "There's been class warfare going on for the last 20 years, and my class has won."

Jamie Dimon, CEO of JPMorgan Chase, 2023 shareholder letter: "America has a growing problem of income inequality… and too many people are being left behind."

They are not ashamed. They are simply stating the scoreboard.

The meritocracy myth survives for one reason: it lets the losers blame themselves.

If you believe the ladder is still there, then the fact that you are exhausted at thirty-five with nothing to show for it must be your fault. You didn't hustle hard enough. You didn't learn to code. You didn't launch the right side gig.

The myth turns private despair into public order.

Meanwhile the real ladder (the one made of inherited trusts, elite preschool admissions, unpaid internships in Manhattan, and seven-figure seed rounds from college roommates) is quietly pulled up behind the last climber.

Capitalism has not become less meritocratic because people suddenly got lazy. It has become less meritocratic because capital, once concentrated, buys better lawyers, better lobbyists, better algorithms, and better politicians to keep it concentrated.

The race is real. The track is tilted ninety degrees. The spectators are told it is flat.

That is the final cruelty of the system: it makes the children of the dispossessed feel morally inferior for losing a game whose rules were rewritten before they were born.

Next, we will look at the only place the myth is still openly defended: inside the boardrooms and the people who actually own the track.

And we will let them speak for themselves. Their honesty will be more damning than any accusation we could invent.

Section: 7. The Verdict from Inside the Machine

They no longer pretend.

Here are the people who own the algorithm, speaking plainly when they think only their peers are listening:

Nick Hanauer (early Amazon investor), 2019 memo to fellow billionaires: "The most important economic and political question facing America today is how do we stop a few billionaires from buying elections and controlling policy… because if we don't, the pitchforks will come."

Ray Dalio (founder of Bridgewater, the world's largest hedge fund), 2021: "I believe that the reason capitalism is in crisis is that it is not providing equal opportunity… The wealth gap and the values gap are at the extremes are the greatest in my lifetime."

Klaus Schwab (World Economic Forum founder), 2016 Davos speech: "The Fourth Industrial Revolution will lead to a fusion of our physical, digital, and biological identities… Many jobs will disappear… We need a new social contract."

World Economic Forum promotional video, 2016 (still on YouTube): "Welcome to 2030. I own nothing, have no privacy, and life has never been better."

Jeff Bezos, 2021 interview after his space joyride: "I want to thank every Amazon employee and every Amazon customer because you guys paid for all this."

Satya Nadella (Microsoft CEO), 2023 internal memo leaked: "We are moving from a world where companies compete for customers to a world where companies compete for scarce labor and scarce capital. The winners will be those who control the platforms."

Jamie Dimon (JPMorgan Chase), 2024 shareholder letter: "America's economic challenges are not cyclical—they are structural… Too many people have been left behind."

Mark Zuckerberg, internal Facebook memo, 2017: "We need to evolve the culture so that people expect that most things they produce will be owned by the company and used to advance our mission."

And finally, the quietest, most chilling admission of all:

BlackRock CEO Larry Fink, 2022 letter to investors: "Stakeholder capitalism is not about politics. It is not a social or ideological agenda. It is capitalism, driven by mutually beneficial relationships between you and the employees, customers, suppliers, and communities your company relies on to prosper… The companies that do this well will be the ones that thrive."

Translation: the peasants must be kept just comfortable enough not to revolt, because the peasants are now the product.

These are not whistle-blowers. These are the architects.

They are not embarrassed by the concentration of ownership. They are proud of it. They are not warning us out of guilt. They are warning us out of self-preservation.

The mask has slipped so far that even the people wearing it no longer bother to adjust it.

Capitalism has achieved its purest victory: a world in which the many own nothing, the few own everything, and the few no longer feel the need to lie about it.

That is the X-ray in full.

The fracture is complete.

The bone has healed crooked.

And the patient is still being told to run faster.

We have seen what unchecked capital does to the family, to the worker, to soul, to future.

The next chapter will show that the socialist alternative, wherever it has been tried, breaks the same bones in almost exactly the same places (only with worse food and longer lines).

Because the wound is not left or right. It is the wound of a world without widespread ownership.

And there is only one known cure.

Chapter 6: Socialism's Children

Section: 1. The Promise This Time

Socialism arrived with a promise even more seductive than capitalism's.

Capitalism had said: "Work hard and one day you will own something." Socialism said: "You will never again have to worry about owning anything. The community, through the state, will own everything for you. No one will be rich, no one will be poor, and every child will be safe."

It sounded like mercy.

The salesmen were passionate. They quoted Marx's line about "from each according to his ability, to each according to his needs" the way priests once quoted the Beatitudes. They promised that once the factories, the land, and the banks belonged to "the people," the ancient curses of poverty, exploitation, and insecurity would vanish forever.

The family, they said, would finally be free, free from the terror of unemployment, free from medical bills, free from the fear that a bad harvest or a factory closure would destroy the next generation.

All that was required was one small sacrifice: hand your property, your tools, your land, your future decisions to the state. The state would become the universal provider, the universal parent, the universal god.

It was a breathtaking offer. Millions took it.

Here is what they actually received.

The property was taken, all right. But it was not handed to "the people." It was handed to a new class: party officials, factory directors, secret policemen, and the bureaucrats who decided what your needs actually were.

The promise quietly changed, the way capitalism's promise had quietly changed a century earlier.

No trumpet blast announced the revision. It simply happened, decree by decree, five-year plan by five-year plan, until the promise now read:

"You will own nothing. The state will own everything. You will be grateful, because the state will take care of you from cradle to grave. And if you are not grateful, the state will still take care of you, only the grave will come sooner."

The compassion was real, for a little while. Then the arithmetic took over.

When no one owns anything, no one has an incentive to care for anything. When no one can say no to the state, the state becomes the only real parent, and parents who cannot be refused eventually become tyrants.

The family was not liberated. It was nationalized.

The next pages will show exactly how that nationalization worked in practice, from Moscow to Havana to Caracas, and why every attempt to make the state the universal owner ended up making the state the universal devourer.

We will look without rage and without nostalgia, the way a pathologist looks at tissue under a microscope.

Because the disease is the same one we saw in Chapter 5, only the symptoms wear a different uniform.

The fracture is identical. Only the flag above the operating table has changed.

Section: 2. The Historical Scorecard

The experiment has been run dozens of times, on every continent, under every conceivable variation ("democratic," "Marxist-Leninist," "African," "21st-century"). The results are now in, and they are brutal.

| Country / Period Promised Outcome/ Actual Outcome
USSR 1917–1991 "From each… to each…"

- 20–60 million dead from famine, purges, gulag
- By 1989 the average Soviet citizen had a lower caloric intake than under the Tsar in 1913
- Elite-to-masses income ratio: top party officials lived in 2025 dollars at $2–5 million lifestyles while workers queued for bread

Maoist China 1949–1976 "Great Leap Forward" to eliminate poverty

- 45–80 million dead in the greatest famine in history (all caused by collectivization)
- Per-capita GDP in 1976: $178 (lower than medieval Europe in wheat-wages)

Cuba 1959–2025 "Socialism or death"

- 2024 per-capita income: ~$1,200 (one-tenth of capitalist Dominican Republic next door)
- 500,000 citizens fled on rafts; 2023–2025: 5 % of the entire population emigrated in two years

Venezuela 1999–2025 "Bolivarian 21st-century socialism"

- Oil wealth nationalized "for the people"
- GDP collapsed 75 %, hyperinflation peaked at 1,700,000 %

- 7.7 million refugees, child malnutrition rates worse than war-torn Yemen

North Korea (1948–today) "Self-reliance"

- Chronic famine, life expectancy 12 years below South Korea
- Top 1 % (party elite) live in Pyongyang palaces while 60 % of the population is undernourished

Even the "success" stories collapse under honest examination:

Sweden / Denmark / Norway Often cited as "proof socialism works" Reality: private ownership of capital is higher than in the U.K. or U.S. Top 10 % own 70–80 % of corporate equity What they actually have is capitalism with very high taxes and very large welfare states—not socialist ownership, just capitalist redistribution.

One table tells the whole story:

Country	**Year Socialism Declared Victory**	**Top 10 % Share of National Income (pre-tax)**	**Bottom 50 % Share**
USSR 1989	1917	35–45 % (party elite)	~20 %
China 2024 (CCP rule)	1949	45–50 % (party-connected)	12–15 %
U.S. 2024 (capitalism)	—	50 %	12 %

Country	Year Socialism Declared Victory	Top 10 % Share of National Income (pre-tax)	Bottom 50 % Share
Sweden 2024	—	40 %	20 %

The numbers are almost identical.

Socialism promised to end the concentration of capital. It delivered the concentration of capital under a different management team.

Capitalism concentrated ownership in corporations and hedge funds. Socialism concentrated ownership in the party, the army, and the secret police.

Both produced a tiny elite that owned almost everything and a vast majority that owned almost nothing.

Both produced collapsing birth rates (Russia 1.1, Cuba 1.0, China 0.9).

Both produced societies where the family could not say no to the central power.

The difference was only in the style of the cage.

Capitalism's cage is gilded and air-conditioned, with Netflix and delivery apps. Socialism's cage was concrete and barbed wire, with longer queues and worse food.

But the cage was still a cage.

The historical record is not ambiguous. It is unanimous.

Every single time the state became the universal owner, the family became the universal dependent.

Next we will walk through the front door of that dependency and see what happened to fathers, mothers, and children when the state declared itself their only provider.

Section: 3. The Family in the Collective

The state that owns everything eventually wants to own the people who will inherit everything. That means it must own the womb, the cradle, and the marriage bed.

The pattern is so consistent across every socialist experiment that it cannot be coincidence.

USSR

- 1920s–1930s: divorce available on a postcard, abortion free and on demand (legalized 1920, before anywhere else in the world).
- 1936: Stalin suddenly re-criminalized abortion and made divorce harder; why? Birth rate had collapsed and the army needed cannon fodder.
- 1944: "bachelor tax" and "childless tax" on men and women who refused to reproduce for the Motherland.
- State nurseries from six weeks old so mothers could meet factory quotas. A woman who stayed home was officially a "parasite." Result: by 1991 the Soviet Union had the highest abortion rate in human history (officially 7–10 abortions per live birth) and the lowest male life expectancy in the developed world.

Maoist China

- 1950s: Marriage Law abolished arranged marriage and gave women the right to divorce (genuine progress).

- 1980–2015: One-Child Policy enforced by forced abortions, forced sterilizations, and fines larger than a worker's lifetime earnings. The state literally decided how many children a family could have, and when. Result: 30–50 million "missing" girls (sex-selective abortion), a male-to-female ratio of 120:100 in many provinces, and today the fastest-ageing population on earth.

Cuba

- Crèches opened at 45 days old.
- Mothers received medals for producing many children for the Revolution, then received pressure to stop when resources ran short.
- 2024 fertility rate: 1.0 (lowest in the Western hemisphere).
- Grandmothers joke that the only thing the Revolution gave them for free was abortion.

East Germany (GDR)

- Full employment for women was compulsory.
- State kindergartens from infancy; children belonged to the state from 8 a.m. to 6 p.m.
- The Stasi kept files on family conversations; children were taught to report "politically unreliable" parents.
- Abortion rate twice that of West Germany. Result: when the Wall fell, East German women's fertility was already 1.3; it dropped further after reunification because the state day-care vanished and housing prices appeared.

Everywhere the same logic played out:

1. The family cannot be allowed to own productive property (it might become independent).
2. Therefore women must work full-time for the state.

3. Therefore children must be raised by the state.
4. Therefore reproduction must be managed by the state.
5. Therefore the family shrinks, ages, and eventually disappears.

The state did not hate the family because it was Marxist. It hated the family because the family is the only institution that can say "no" to the state without asking permission.

Once the household owns nothing that produces wealth, it has no leverage, no refuge, no future except the one the state hands out.

The compassion was real in the beginning. The arithmetic was merciless in the end.

A system that owns all capital must eventually own all time, all loyalty, and all children.

The promise was: "You will be free from the tyranny of property." The reality was: "You will be property."

Next we will walk through the door of a Soviet apartment, a Chinese village compound, a Cuban ration line, and see what daily life felt like when the state had successfully become the only father your children would ever know.

Section: 4. The New Socialist Serfdom

The capitalist serf can, in theory, quit his job, move cities, or start a side hustle. The socialist serf could not even change apartments without written permission.

The difference was not rhetorical. It was enforced by documents, walls, and guns.

USSR

- Every citizen carried an internal passport.

- Leaving your assigned city without a stamp was a criminal offence.
- Your propiska (residential permit) decided where your children could go to school and whether you could buy bread.
- Your labor book of labor recorded every job; quitting without approval meant losing housing, rations, and pension rights.
- Housing was "free" but allocated by the state; a family of four typically received 9–14 square meters total (one small room plus kitchen).

China (pre-1990s hukou system, still partially in force)

- Rural citizens were legally tied to their village and forbidden to move to cities.
- Urban citizens received grain coupons, housing, and medical care; rural citizens received nothing but the obligation to sell crops to the state at fixed prices.
- Until 2014 a rural mother who married an urban man still could not bring her children into the city legally.

Cuba

- Until 2013 you needed Ministry of Interior permission to change homes inside the same city.
- Selling your apartment was illegal until 2011.
- Leaving the island without an exit visa was punishable by prison.

East Germany

- The Berlin Wall was officially called the "Anti-Fascist Protection Rampart." Its real purpose was to stop citizens from voting with their feet. Three million had already fled westward before it went up.

North Korea (today)

- Citizens are classified at birth into songbun castes.
- Moving to another province without state approval is treason.
- Three generations are punished for one person's attempt to escape.

This was not a side effect. It was the system working exactly as designed.

When the state owns all productive property, it cannot allow labor to move freely. Free movement would create labor shortages, wage pressure, and (worst of all) comparison. If the workers in Factory A discover that workers in Factory B have meat twice a week, the plan collapses.

So the state binds the worker to his place with the same chains the medieval lord once used (only now the chains are made of paper, barbed wire, and secret-police files).

The socialist serf was legally freer than the medieval serf (no hereditary status, no corvée labor in theory). He was practically far less free.

The medieval serf could not be moved off his strip. The socialist citizen could not move onto a better one.

The medieval serf owed three days a week to the lord. The socialist citizen owed seven days a week to the state (and was told it was voluntary).

The medieval serf could be beaten but not easily killed. The socialist serf could be worked to death in a labor camp for "economic sabotage" if he missed his quota.

And when the system began to crack (1989–1991), the first thing millions did was exactly what capitalism's gig workers now dream of doing: they ran.

They ran so fast that the Berlin Wall had to be torn down by hand to keep the guards from being trampled.

The socialist serfdom was never abolished by reform. It was abandoned by escape.

Today the cage is softer in Beijing and Havana (tourism dollars and remittances keep it painted), but the legal structure is still there, ready to be tightened the moment the subsidies run out.

The promise was: "No more masters." The reality was: one master, permanent and unchangeable.

Next we will step inside the soul of the person who lived under that master, and see what happens to hope when even your children belong to the state.

The wound is the same wound we saw under capitalism. Only the anesthetic was different.

Section: 5. The Spiritual Wound, Part II

The money was taken first. The soul was taken next.

When the state owns everything, it does not merely own your labor. It owns your future, your children's future, and therefore your hope.

The wound shows itself in small, ordinary moments that no statistic can catch.

It is the Soviet engineer who spends his evenings standing in line for potatoes, then drinks himself to sleep because tomorrow will be the same line, only longer.

It is the Cuban grandmother who teaches her grandson to say "thank you, Fidel" for the single egg ration, because the walls have ears.

It is the East German mother who discovers her twelve-year-old has written a school essay denouncing her for listening to Western radio, and realizes the child believes he is doing the right thing.

It is the Chinese father in 1989 who tells his daughter, "Study English, marry a foreigner, get out," because he no longer believes the system will ever allow a normal life.

Hope did not die in a single dramatic moment. It died by a thousand small calculations:

- "If I speak up, I lose my job, my apartment, my children's university place."
- "If I work harder, the quota only goes up."
- "If I have another child, the fine will bankrupt us and the child will be punished forever."

The wound has a color: grey. The wound has a smell: boiled cabbage and cheap vodka, and fear.

Visitors to late-socialist cities always used the same words: "Everyone looks twenty years older than they are." The body survived; the soul aged in dog years.

Charity died first. When the state declares itself the only giver, private generosity becomes suspect. Why would you help your neighbor when the state is supposed to do it? Why would you start a business when the state will take it? Why would you fix the roof when the building belongs to no one?

Initiative died next. The Russian proverb from the 1970s sums it up: "They pretend to pay us, we pretend to work."

Faith died slowly. Churches were turned into warehouses, priests into informants, Christmas into "Winter Festival." The family was the last remaining church, so the state infiltrated it with informers, quotas, and compulsory atheism classes.

The wound shows most clearly in the birth rates. When people lose the conviction that their children can have a better life, they stop having children. Every socialist country reached replacement level fertility and then fell below it faster than any capitalist country in history.

Russia today: 1.1 Ukraine: 1.0 Cuba: 1.0 China (post-one-child): 0.9 and still falling

The state had promised to be the perfect parent. It became the parent that eats its young.

The survivors speak with one voice.

Vaclav Havel, dissident turned president: "The worst thing is that we learned to live without hope."

Solzhenitsyn, after the camps: "The socialist state is a machine for crushing the human spirit. It succeeds."

A Cuban exile in Miami, 2023: "In Havana they gave us free schools and free doctors. In Miami I pay for everything, but for the first time in my life I feel like a man."

The spiritual wound under socialism was not louder than under capitalism. It was deeper, because there was no legal escape, no side hustle, no lottery ticket fantasy of getting rich and moving to Florida.

There was only the state, forever.

And the state did not love you back.

The wound is the same wound we saw in Chapter 5: the wound of a human being reduced to a dependent who owns nothing productive.

Only this time the landlord wore a red star instead of a logo, and the eviction notice was written in bureaucratic prose instead of an app notification.

The family was not freed from property. It was freed from hope.

Next we will stand back and watch the two systems (capitalist and socialist) walk toward each other across a century and finally embrace, like long-lost brothers who discover they have been wearing different uniforms but carrying the same gun.

The convergence is almost complete. And the family is still in the middle.

Section: 6. The Convergence

Stand on any street corner in 2025 and look carefully. You will see two systems that spent a century screaming at each other now quietly shaking hands behind the curtain.

Late-stage capitalism and late-stage socialism have arrived at the same destination, by different roads, wearing different costumes.

Compare the columns:

Feature	Late-Stage Capitalism (2025)	Late-Stage Socialism (China 2025 / Cuba 2025)
Who owns productive capital	Tiny private elite + index funds	Party-connected elite + state

Feature	Late-Stage Capitalism (2025)	Late-Stage Socialism (China 2025 / Cuba 2025)
		corporations
Who decides housing allocation	Algorithm + BlackRock	Hukou system + party committee
Who controls movement	Credit score + rental history	Social-credit score + internal passport
Who monitors daily behaviour	Phone apps + Ring cameras	WeChat + facial-recognition cameras
Fertility rate	1.6 (U.S.)	0.9 (China)
Typical family owns	Debt, subscriptions, a phone	Debt to the state, a ration book
Can you quit and start your own thing?	Theoretically yes, practically almost never	Theoretically never, practically almost never
Elite-to-masses income ratio	344:1 (U.S. CEO vs worker)	300–500:1 (Chinese billionaire vs migrant)
The dream sold to the young	"One day you'll be rich"	"One day the nation will be rich"
The reality	You will own	You will own

Feature	Late-Stage Capitalism (2025)	Late-Stage Socialism (China 2025 / Cuba 2025)
delivered	nothing and stream content	nothing and serve the collective glory

The uniforms are different—one wears a hoodie and flies private, the other wears a Zhongshan suit and flies Air China First Class—but the body underneath is the same.

Both systems have achieved what Belloc predicted in 1912: a small owning class and a large dependent class, legally separated by a maze of permissions, scores, and algorithms.

Both systems have turned the family into a consumption unit (capitalism) or a production unit (socialism), never an ownership unit.

Both systems have made children so expensive, in money or in risk, that most couples quietly decide the species ends with them.

Both systems watch you constantly, reward compliance, punish independence, and call it "modernization."

The only real disagreement left is branding.

One side calls the cage "freedom." The other side calls it "harmony." The bars are equally cold.

Even the language has converged. Read a 2024 World Economic Forum white paper next to a 2024 Chinese Communist Party economic resolution. Both speak of "stakeholder governance," "public-private partnerships," "digital inclusion," and "sustainable development goals." Both assume that large platforms (corporate or state) will own the infrastructure while citizens enjoy "access."

BlackRock and the Chinese Communist Party now co-invest in the same projects. Silicon Valley billionaires praise Xi's efficiency. European socialists praise Singapore's (state-capitalist) model.

Capitalism did not defeat socialism. Socialism did not defeat capitalism. Together they defeated the family, the small owner, and the human scale.

And together they built the Servile State Belloc warned about: a society in which almost everything that produces wealth is owned by a merged public-private elite, and almost everyone else is a well-fed, well-tracked, well-medicated dependent.

The flags are different. The fracture is identical.

Next, in short summary, we will let the people who lived under the red flag speak the verdict that the people under the rainbow flag are only now beginning to whisper.

Their words will be the bridge to the only door still open.

Section: 7. The Quiet Confession of the Survivors

The people who lived under the red flag do not shout anymore. They speak softly, because they know what happens when you shout at the state.

Vaclav Havel, 1978, from a prison cell: "The line between good and evil does not run between systems, but through every human heart. But a system that owns everything makes it almost impossible for the good to win."

Aleksandr Solzhenitsyn, 1974, expelled from his country: "Socialism of any type leads to a total destruction of the human spirit and to a levelling of mankind into death."

Xi Van Fleet, survivor of Mao's Cultural Revolution, speaking in Virginia, 2021: "I lived socialism. You are being told it is compassion. It is control. The state becomes your parent, your teacher, your god. And it never gives you back your freedom."

A Cuban doctor who fled in 2023: "They gave us free medicine and free schools. But they took our future. My daughter will never own the clinic she works in. She will never own the apartment she lives in. She will only own the right to leave—if they let her."

A former East German teacher, 2019: "We were told we were building paradise. We built a prison with better wallpaper. When the Wall fell, the first thing we did was cry—not for joy, but because we realized how much of our lives had been stolen."

Even the true believers who never repented admit the failure in their own way.

Fidel Castro, 2005, asked about the Cuban model: "The Cuban model doesn't even work for us anymore."

Modern European socialists, when pressed in private: "We learned the hard way that you cannot redistribute what nobody owns. Without widespread private property, there is nothing to tax and nothing to share."

They promised the family would be freed from the tyranny of property. They delivered the family from hope.

The survivors do not ask for pity. They ask for honesty.

They have seen the end of the road we are still walking. They have lived the convergence we are only now noticing.

And they all say the same thing, in different accents:

Do not give the state what belongs to the family. Do not give the corporation what belongs to the family. Because whoever owns the future owns the children.

The cage-fight is over. The promoters have merged. The audience is still in the stands, arguing about which fighter was better.

Meanwhile the third door, the one they told us was bricked up—has been standing open the whole time.

We have seen what capitalism does to the family when capital is concentrated. We have seen what socialism does to the family when the state is concentrated.

Both deliver servitude. One with a smile and a subscription. One with a uniform and a quota.

There is only one alternative left.

It is older than both systems. It has never been refuted. It has only been forgotten.

Let us turn the page. The distributist difference is waiting.

Chapter 7: The Distributist Difference

Section: 1. The One Thing Both Systems Got Wrong

Capitalism and socialism spent a century shouting at each other across a battlefield, and the entire time they were standing on the same patch of ground.

They agreed on one non-negotiable premise:

Productive property (land, tools, machines, code, equity) must be concentrated in a few hands. They only disagreed about whose hands.

Capitalism said: "Let it concentrate in private corporations and hedge funds. The invisible hand will eventually trickle the benefits downward." Socialism said: "Let it concentrate in the state and its agencies. The visible hand will distribute the benefits fairly."

Both were wrong about the premise.

The premise itself is the disease.

When productive property is concentrated (whether in boardrooms or bureaucracies), the result is always the same:

- A small owning class
- A large dependent class
- A family that cannot say no to whoever controls the capital

- Children who inherit debt and subscriptions instead of tools and land
- A civilization that slowly stops having children because it no longer believes in a future worth owning

Distributism does not argue about which elite should own the concentrated capital. It rejects the concentration itself.

It starts from the opposite premise, the one written into Genesis, Aristotle, Aquinas, the medieval village, and the human heart:

Productive property should be distributed (as widely as possible, to as many families as possible, in forms they can actually use and pass on).

Not because it is sentimental. Because it is the only arrangement that has ever produced free men, fertile families, and cultures worth living in.

Capitalism promised freedom and delivered wage-dependence for the many, monopoly for the few. Socialism promised equality and delivered state-dependence for the many, monopoly for the party.

Distributism promises neither freedom nor equality in the abstract. It promises the only thing that ever actually delivered both: ownership.

Not luxury. Not utopia. Just the normal human condition that existed for most of history until we decided, in a fit of ideological madness, that concentrating capital was "progress."

The concentration was the original sin of the modern world.

Everything we have suffered since (the exhausted parents, the childless cities, the gig serfs, the concrete cages, the collapse of hope) is simply the interest on that sin.

Distributism is not a new idea. It is the oldest idea: that a man and woman and their children should own enough of the world to live in it without selling their freedom every morning.

The next pages will show you what happens when that idea is put into practice.

It works. It works so well that once you see it, you will never again understand how we let ourselves be talked out of it.

Section: 2. The Core Principle in One Sentence

Here is the entire distributist programmed, small enough to fit on a postcard and large enough to rebuild civilization:

As many families as possible should own enough productive property to live in reasonable security and genuine freedom, without either corporate monopoly or state bureaucracy.

Now let us unpack the sentence word by word, the way you unpack a suitcase after a long exile and discover everything you need is still inside.

"As many families as possible" Not every single family (there will always be the young, the sick, the unlucky). But the overwhelming majority. The default condition of a healthy society should be ownership, not tenancy, employment, or welfare.

"should own" Not rent, not lease, not subscribe, not have theoretical access to. Own. In the full, old, fierce sense: the legal and practical ability to use it, improve it, defend it, and hand it to their children.

"enough productive property" Not luxury. Not a yacht. But something that actually produces wealth while they sleep: a house with a garden, a share in the company they work for, a small farm, a workshop, a co-op bakery, a few acres of timber, a solar array on the roof, a fishing boat, a software partnership.

Enough to keep body and soul together if the boss fires them or the algorithm deactivates them.

"to live in reasonable security" Not bulletproof certainty (nothing is). But the kind of security that lets a father look his children in the eye and say, "As long as I have strength, no one will take this roof from us."

"and genuine freedom" The freedom to say no. No to the landlord who raises the rent 40 %. No to the employer who demands 70-hour weeks. No to the state that wants to educate your children in things you believe are evil. Freedom that comes from having an alternative, not from having a louder voice on social media.

"without either corporate monopoly" No more Amazon, BlackRock, or Vanguard owning half the economy. No single entity so large that it can dictate terms to entire nations.

"or state bureaucracy" No more five-year plans, social-credit scores, or ministries deciding who gets a building permit and who gets a labor camp.

That is the whole thing.

Everything else (tax policy, co-ops, land reform, ESOP laws) is just plumbing.

The principle is older than left and right. It is the principle of the Passover lamb eaten in a house marked with blood, of the Jubilee trumpet returning every man to his vineyard, of the carpenter in Nazareth who owned His tools and set His own hours.

It is the principle that made medieval villages sing, that made the Basque valleys unbreakable, that is making Mondragón and Cleveland and Taiwan rich while the rest of the world argues about which form of concentration is less bad.

It is not complicated. It is only unfamiliar because we have spent two centuries being told that concentration is inevitable.

It is not inevitable. It is a choice.

And the moment enough families choose the opposite, the whole modern arrangement (debt, despair, demographic winter) begins to crumble like a sandcastle at high tide.

The next pages will show you the tools that are already in our hands, the places that are already using them, and the family that is already being saved by them.

You will not need a revolution. You will only need to remember what human life looked like before we forgot.

The sentence is short. The consequences are endless.

Section: 3. The Tools That Already Exist

You do not need to invent anything new. The tools are on the shelf, tested, legal in most countries, and working right now. Pick one up and start.

1. Employee Stock Ownership Plans (ESOPs) A company sells some or all of its shares into a trust owned by the workers. The workers pay nothing up front; the company pays the trust with future profits. Result: every employee becomes an owner without taking on personal debt. Already used by 6,500 U.S. companies, 14 million worker-owners, $1.9 trillion in assets. Example: Publix supermarkets (230,000 worker-owners) and WinCo Foods regularly beat Walmart on wages and customer satisfaction while remaining 100 % employee-owned.
2. Worker Cooperatives The workers own the company outright, one member one vote. Mondragón (80,000

owners), Emilia-Romagna (one-third of regional GDP), the 300+ U.S. food co-ops that survived Covid better than any chain. Start-up recipe: 5–15 people, a good product, a credit-union loan, and a lawyer who knows co-op statutes (most states have them).

3. Community Land Trusts & Limited-Equity Housing Co-ops The land is bought by a non-profit trust and leased to families at low cost forever. The house can be sold, but only at an inflation-adjusted price, so it stays affordable for the next family. Over 500,000 Americans already live in such housing; new trusts are forming every month in cities where hedge funds are pricing teachers and nurses out.
4. Credit Unions and Mutual Banks Member-owned banks that lend only to members for productive purposes. In the U.S. they hold $2.3 trillion and charge half the fees of big banks. In Germany and Austria the Raiffeisen network still finances most small farms and shops. Join one tomorrow; start one the day after if yours doesn't exist.
5. Family-Farm Succession Laws & Agricultural Co-ops Tax breaks and low-interest loans for transferring the farm or business to the next generation. Used in Japan, France, and Taiwan to keep family ownership above 90 %. In the U.S., state-level "beginning farmer" programmers and the Farm Service Agency will lend you 100 % of a farm purchase if you have five years' experience.
6. Micro-Land Trusts and Homestead Funds Churches, unions, and neighborhood groups buy one house or one acre at a time, put it into perpetual trust, and lease it to a working family for $200–$400 a month. Already happening in Detroit, Atlanta, Belfast, and rural Vermont.

7. Local Currencies and Mutual Credit Systems Bristol Pound, Sardex (Sardinia), WIR (Switzerland): businesses issue credit to each other, bypassing banks entirely. WIR has kept Swiss small firms alive through every recession since 1934.

Every one of these tools is legal today in most places on earth. Every one has a website, a phone number, and people who will answer your questions for free.

You do not need to wait for a new law, a new party, or a new pope. You need to pick up the tool that fits your hand and start swinging.

In the next section after next we will watch seven ordinary families (one for each tool) walk out of the cage and into daylight. But first, let us take a quick world tour and see the places that are already living proof.

Section: 4. Red Toryism: A Modern Echo in Conservative Thought

Distributism's English roots have never truly died; they have simply found new voices in new generations.

In the first decade of the twenty-first century, Anglican theologian and political philosopher Phillip Blond gave those roots fresh soil in a book called *Red Tory: How Left and Right Have Broken Britain and How We Can Fix It* (2010). Blond looked at a Britain hollowed out by thirty years of neoliberal economics on one side and statist managerialism on the other. He saw the same twin predators that Chesterton and Belloc had named a century earlier: a market that concentrates wealth in ever-fewer corporate hands, and a state that concentrates power in ever-larger bureaucracies. Both, he argued, erode the very institutions that make human life thick and meaningful—families, neighborhoods, voluntary associations, churches, mutual societies, small businesses.

His diagnosis was unmistakably distributist in spirit: the problem is not markets or welfare as such, but the *concentration* of capital and decision-making in distant hands. The solution, he proposed, is a "civic state" that actively dismantles monopolies, breaks up oligarchic control of land and finance, and deliberately cultivates widespread ownership—through mutual ownership models, employee stakes, community land trusts, credit unions, co-operatives, and policies that favor local and family-scale enterprise over distant corporate or bureaucratic giants.

Blond drew explicitly from Chesterton and Belloc. He praised their vision of a nation of owners rather than renters or dependents. He echoed their suspicion of both laissez-faire capitalism (which turns citizens into consumers) and Fabian socialism (which turns them into clients). Yet he adapted the vision for a post-industrial, post-Christian Britain. Where classic distributism often emphasized radical subsidiarity and a minimal state once ownership is diffused, Red Toryism envisions a more muscular "civic state" that uses public power to rebuild intermediary institutions, guarantee basic welfare without creating dependency, and restore a shared moral and cultural life. It is less purist about state restraint and more pragmatic about using government as a temporary scaffold to rebuild civil society.

The influence was real, if partial. David Cameron's "Big Society" agenda in the early 2010s borrowed heavily from Blond's ideas. It promoted mutuals, co-ops, community ownership, and voluntary associations as alternatives to both market fundamentalism and top-down bureaucracy. Though the execution was uneven and underfunded, the intellectual DNA was clear: distributist principles could still inspire centre-right politics in a secular age.

For Anglicans, Red Toryism offers a particularly resonant bridge. Rooted in the Anglo-Catholic tradition of social concern (F.D. Maurice, Charles Gore, William Temple), it speaks the language of virtue, tradition, and the common good without requiring Catholic doctrinal commitments. It proves that the distributist impulse of widespread ownership, local flourishing, and moral limits on power is not confined to one confession or one century. It lives wherever people still believe that a good society is built from the household upward, not from the boardroom or the ministry downward.

Red Toryism is not identical to distributism. It allows a more active state role in fostering civic renewal than the stricter subsidiarity of Leo XIII or Chesterton. But that difference only underscores the living power of the underlying principle: when ordinary families own enough to live in decency and independence, the cage-fight between red corner and blue corner loses its audience. The household republic begins to rise again—even in the language of twenty-first-century conservatism.

Section: 5. Seven Living Proofs You Can Visit Today

You do not need to take my word for any of this. Book a flight, rent a car, knock on doors. These places will let you touch the evidence with your own hands.

1. Mondragón, Basque Country, Spain
   Population of the valley: 90,000. Unemployment: 2.8 %. Largest supermarket chain, largest appliance manufacturer, and one of the world's top automotive

suppliers—all worker-owned. Walk into any Eroski supermarket and ask an employee who owns the store. They will point to themselves and say, "We do." They are not waiting for permission. They are doing it.

2. Emilia-Romagna, Italy
   From Bologna to Rimini: one-third of GDP from cooperatives. Highest per-capita income in Italy, lowest youth unemployment in Europe, birth rate 30 % above the Italian average. Go to a Parma ham factory; the workers slicing the prosciutto own the building, the brand, and the profits. They are not waiting for permission. They are doing it.
3. The ESOP Belt – Ohio, Kansas, Midwest U.S.
   Drive an hour outside any mid-size city and you will pass companies you have never heard of that are 100 % employee-owned: engineering firms, manufacturers, grocery chains. Stop at the headquarters, ask to see the retirement statements. The forklift driver you meet will have $400,000–$1 million in company stock. They are not waiting for permission. They are doing it.
4. Taiwan
   99.8 % of businesses have fewer than 200 employees. Average firm size: six people. Yet they make half the world's advanced semiconductors. Visit a night market; every stall is a family firm that owns its recipe, its location, and its future. They are not waiting for permission. They are doing it.
5. Kerala, India
   One of the poorest states in India has the highest life expectancy, and literacy in the country. Because one-third of the population belongs to a cooperative (hospitals,

banks, schools, coconut factories). Sit in a Kudumbashree meeting and watch 20 former maids decide how to spend their own profits. They are not waiting for permission. They are doing it.

6. The Tyrol, Austria/Northern Italy
   Mountain valleys where almost every farm is still family-owned, thanks to inheritance laws that keep land from being swallowed by corporations. Highest density of small hotels, micro-breweries, and artisan cheesemakers in Europe. Children still learn the family trade before university. They are not waiting for permission. They are doing it.
7. Cleveland, Ohio – Evergreen Cooperatives
   In one of America's poorest neighborhoods, ex-prisoners and single mothers now own a solar-installation company, an industrial laundry serving hospitals, and a greenhouse that supplies salad to universities. All 100 % worker-owned, all profitable, all growing. Walk into the laundry at 7 a.m. and ask who the boss is. The woman running the folding machine will smile and say, "We all are." They are not waiting for permission. They are doing it.

Seven places. Seven places of proof.

None of them is perfect. All of them are freer, richer, and more fertile than the places that surround them.

All of them began with a handful of people who got tired of waiting for the "realistic" solutions and simply started owning things again.

You can visit any of them next year. You can copy any of them next month.

The revolution is not coming. It is already here, and waiting for company.

Next we will take the exhausted family from the very first page of this book and walk them, step by step, out of the cage and into one of these living proofs.

You will watch their budget balance, their sleep return, and their children laugh again.

Because the difference is not theoretical. It is biographical.

Section: 6. The Family That Ownership Saves

Go back to the house we visited in the Introduction. It is still Tuesday evening, 2026. The rent notice is still sits on the counter. The father is still staring at a $312 bank balance. But this time the story does not end there.

Watch what happens when the distributist tools we just met are quietly put into their hands.

Year 1 – The Warehouse Becomes Theirs The father's employer (a 2.2-million-square-foot distribution center bought out by an ESOP. The retiring owner sells 100 % of the shares to the workers on a fifteen-year note. No money leaves the father's pocket. Within five years he owns shares worth $180,000 on top of his wage. The company now pays annual profit-sharing bonuses because there are no outside shareholders to bleed it dry. His take-home pay rises 22 % without a single extra hour.

Year 2 – The House They Will Never Lose They join a new community land trust forming in their county. They buy a modest three-bedroom house with a half-acre lot for $185,000 (the trust owns the land, they own the house). Ground lease: $75 a month forever. Mortgage payment: $1,100 instead of the $2,400 rent they were paying. They plant fruit trees and a big garden beds the first spring. By year four the garden and a few laying hens cut their grocery bill by $400 a month.

Year 3 – Mom Comes Home The mother, a trained midwife, joins six other midwives to form a worker co-op. They rent a small birth center with a credit-union financing. Because they own the practice, they set their own hours. She drops to three shifts a week and is home for bedtime four nights out of seven. The co-op clears enough profit that every midwife takes home 30 % more than the hospital had paid them.

Year 5 – The Children Inheritances Begin The father's shares are now worth $320,000. The mother's co-op buys the birth-center building outright. They pay off the house mortgage early. Total net worth (not counting the land trust lease) passes $700,000. Their combined work week is 55 hours instead of 90. They welcome a third child (something they had thought financially impossible).

Year 10 – The Future Is No Longer Borrowed The children are 18, 15, and 10. The eldest is already a voting member of the ESOP and learning welding in the company training program. The middle child works weekends at the midwife co-op's herb garden (another co-op venture). The youngest helps in the family orchard that now sells direct to neighbors and the local food co-op.

Their monthly budget in year 10 looks like this:

Category	2026 (rented life)	2036 (owned life)
Housing	$2,400	$75 (land lease)
Food	$1,200	$450
Transport	$900	$400

Category	2026 (rented life)	2036 (owned life)
Health	$1,100	$1,900 (profit shares + co-op draw)
Total work hours/week	90+	55
Sleep per night	5.5 hours	7.5 hours
Children	2 (and terrified of a third)	3 (and talking about a fourth)

They still live in the same town. They still drive used cars. They are not rich by magazine standards.

But they own.

They own the roof, the trees, the shares, the practice, the future. No one can raise their rent 40 %. No algorithm can deactivate them at 3 a.m. No five-year plan can tell them how many children to have.

They have become what every healthy civilization once took for granted: a free family.

The father, now forty-two, says the sentence he never thought he would say: "If something happens to me, my wife and children will still be safe."

The mother, rocking the new baby on the porch they built themselves, answers: "And if something happens to both of us, the children will still own the orchard and the shares. They will never have to start from zero."

That sentence is the entire revolution.

It is not a slogan. It is a life.

And it is built with tools that exist right now, in your country, probably in your county.

The family from 2026 is not a fairy tale. They are the statistical composite of thousands of real families who have already walked this path.

You can meet them at the Mondragón assembly line, the Cleveland laundry, the Tyrolean dairy, the Kerala women's co-op meeting.

They are not waiting for perfect conditions. They are simply refusing to stay tenants any longer.

Next we will face the chorus of professional sceptics who will insist this is all very nice but impossible.

We will answer them one by one, with receipts.

Because the evidence is no longer theoretical. It is walking around on two legs, raising children, and laughing at the people who told them it could not be done.

Section: 7. Answering the "Yeah, But…" Chorus

The sceptics have had a hundred years of practice. Their objections arrive in the same order every time. Here they are, with the answers the sceptics never want you to hear.

"Yeah, but it can't scale." Mondragón: 80,000 worker-owners, €12 billion revenue, exports to 150 countries, still governed by one-member-one-vote. Emilia-Romagna: 1.5 million co-operators producing one-third of a G8 region's GDP. Taiwan: 23 million people, 99.8 % of firms under 200 employees, 12th-richest economy on earth. Scale achieved.

"Yeah, but people are too selfish/greedy/lazy." U.S. credit unions (member-owned) have higher customer-satisfaction scores than any big bank and survived 2008 with almost zero failures. ESOP companies lay people off at one-third the rate of conventional firms, because the workers literally own the buffer. Selfishness turns into stewardship the moment people have skin in the game.

"Yeah, but it's nostalgic/romantic/backward-looking." Taiwan went from rice paddies to semiconductors in forty years using small-firm distributist policies. Cleveland's Evergreen Cooperatives installed solar panels and industrial laundries in the 21st century, not the 19th. Nostalgia is irrelevant; results are not.

"Yeah, but it only works in Catholic/Latin/Basque cultures." Most successful examples:

- Taiwan: Confucian/Buddhist
- Japan: Shinto/secular
- Denmark: Lutheran
- Kerala: Hindu/Muslim/Christian mix
- U.S. Midwest ESOPs: overwhelmingly Protestant The principle travels better than Marxism ever did.

"Yeah, but the market will always out-compete small owners." Worker-owned firms show 2–4 % higher productivity than investor-owned peers (same technology, same market). They survive recessions better because they cut dividends before they cut jobs. Italian co-ops gained market share every year of the 2008–2018 crisis while conventional firms shrank.

"Yeah, but big corporations have economies of scale." Small-firm districts (Emilia-Romagna, Taiwan, southern Germany) consistently out-innovate and out-export corporate giants in everything from machine tools to fashion to precision electronics. Flexibility and skin-in-the-game beat bureaucratic scale every time.

"Yeah, but modern technology requires massive capital concentration." The most advanced chip factories on earth (TSMC in Taiwan) are supplied by thousands of small and medium family firms making specialized parts. Open-source software (Linux, Wikipedia, Apache) is built by distributed ownership and runs 96 % of the world's top one million servers. Concentration is a choice, not a law of physics.

"Yeah, but the government will never allow it." Every tool in Section 3 is already legal in most countries. ESOP tax breaks were passed by the U.S. Congress in 1974 and expanded under Reagan, Clinton, and Trump. Italian co-op laws were written by Christian Democrats and Socialists together. The government only stops you if you wait for permission instead of starting.

"Yeah, but it's too late—the billionaires already own everything." They own a lot, not everything. There are still 30 million small businesses in the U.S. alone, 300 million family farms worldwide, and trillions in pension funds that can be steered into worker buyouts tomorrow. The game is not over; it has barely started.

The chorus has been wrong every single time it opened its mouth for the last hundred years. It was wrong about the medieval guilds, wrong about the Irish land reform, wrong about Mondragón, wrong about Taiwan, wrong about ESOPs.

It is still wrong.

The only thing the chorus has ever been right about is this: if you keep listening to it, nothing will change.

Open your eyes.

The evidence is walking around on two legs, raising children, paying no rent to hedge funds, and sleeping through the night.

They are not arguing with the chorus anymore. They are too busy living.

Next, one short, lyrical pause to remember why any of this matters at all. Because ownership does not only save bank accounts.

Section: 8. The Beauty That Only Ownership Unlocks

When families own again, something happens that no government program and no corporation can fake.

The world stops being a product and becomes a gift again.

The father comes home from the co-op meeting with dirt under his nails from the community orchard he helped plant. He is tired, but he is smiling the way only a man smiles when the tree is his and the fruit will be his children's.

The mother hangs laundry on a line she strung herself, between two apple trees she grafted last spring. The sheets smell of sun and wind, not of the dryer sheets she used to buy because the laundromat ate her quarters.

On Friday evening the neighbors walk over without texting first. Someone brings a guitar, someone brings bread still warm from the outdoor oven they built together. The children chase fireflies while the adults argue about whose turn it is to host next week's feast day.

No one is live-streaming it. No one is monetizing it. It is simply happening, the way festivals used to happen before they became sponsored content.

Work slows down because it no longer has to be squeezed for every last cent of someone else's profit. There is time to plane a door by hand, to carve a spoon for the new baby, to teach the ten-year-old how to tune the old truck so it will still run when he is thirty.

The Sabbath returns, not as a luxury, but as a fact written into the ownership papers: the land rests, the workshop closes, the co-op votes to shut the machines from Saturday night to Monday morning because the members have decided that souls matter more than throughput.

Beauty returns because ugliness is no longer profitable. No one builds particle-board houses when the buyers are the same people who will live in them for three generations. No one sprays poison on the orchard when the children eat the fruit straight from the tree.

The songs come back—the old ones nobody wrote down, the new ones made up on the porch. The stories come back—the ones about how Grandfather bought the back forty with a $400 loan from the credit union in 1962, the ones that end "and now it's yours."

Leisure returns, the real kind that Josef Pieper said is the basis of culture. Not the exhausted collapse in front of a screen, but the quiet contemplation that is possible only when you are no longer afraid of Monday morning.

A civilization of owners does not need to be entertained every second. It is too busy making things worth looking at, worth listening to, worth passing on.

Chesterton said the world would be saved by beauty. He was right. But beauty is never cheap. It is the first casualty of a society that must extract maximum profit from every square inch and every waking minute.

Ownership restores the margin where beauty grows.

Walk through Mondragón on a feast day, or an Emilia-Romagna village on Sunday afternoon, or a Tyrolean valley at dusk, and you will see it: streets full of children, tables set in the open air, old men arguing about politics and young men arguing about nothing, churches full, workshops closed, music drifting from open windows.

It is not an advertisement. It is the natural environment of the free human being.

We were not made to be efficient. We were made to be fruitful.

Ownership is the soil in which fruitfulness grows back.

The numbers matter, the budgets matter, the tools matter. But this is why they matter.

Because when the family owns again, the world becomes worth inheriting again.

And when the world is worth inheriting, people start having children again.

That is the beauty no algorithm can calculate and no state can decree.

It can only be grown, one free household at a time.

And it is already growing.

Section: 9. Starting Where You Stand

You do not need a majority. You do not need a manifesto. You only need to begin.

Here are ten things you can do next week (most of them cost nothing except courage):

1. Move your money to a credit union or mutual bank. If you are in the U.S., go to www.ncua.gov and find one within ten miles. Do it Monday morning.
2. Find out if your company's ESOP status. Ask HR: "Does the owner have a succession plan?" If the answer is "I don't know," send them the one-page ESOP fact sheet (it exists; I'll give you the link).
3. Start or join a buying club with five neighbors. One bulk order of rice, beans, chicken, and toilet paper per month saves every family $150–$300. Turn the savings into the first payment on a community land-trust house.
4. Plant something that outlives you. A fruit tree, a grape vine, a walnut. Even in a rental yard you can plant in pots and take them when you go.
5. Teach your child (or yourself) one marketable trade that cannot be fully automated. Welding, plumbing, midwifery, small-engine repair, cheese-making, coding for local businesses. One skill that can be practiced from a home shop or co-op.
6. Look up the community land trusts or limited-equity co-ops in your region. If none exist, download the standard legal template (it's free) and call the first meeting in your living room.
7. Switch one bill to a cooperative alternative. (Preferably Christian one) Electricity (co-op utilities serve 42 million Americans), internet (hundreds of rural fiber co-ops), insurance (mutual companies).
8. Refuse one form of predatory finance this year. Pay off the highest-interest credit card, cancel the subscription you don't use, say no to the next year's iPhone upgrade.

9. Tell three people what you just read. Not to argue—just to plant the seed. Revolutions begin in conversations that feel like gossip.
10. Pray the only distributist prayer you will ever need: "Lord, make us dangerous to the concentration of wealth, gentle to the poor, and faithful to the land You gave us. Amen."

Do one of these tomorrow. Do three by Christmas. Do all ten by next year.

The revolution will not be subsidized. It will not be tweeted. It will not be led by a charismatic billionaire or a five-year plan.

It will be inherited, one household at a time.

One family that stops renting its future. One workshop that buys out the retiring owner. One orchard that feeds four generations. One street where the houses are owned by the people who rock babies on the porches.

That is how the medieval village came back to life in the Tyrol. That is how Mondragón grew from five men in a garage. That is how the exhausted family in Chapter 5 became the free family in Chapter 7.

The door is not at the end of history. The door is right behind you.

All you have to do is turn the handle.

Chapter 8: Beauty, Sabbath, and the Leisure of Ownership

Section: 1. The Forgotten Hunger

There is a hunger that no salary can satisfy and no welfare cheque can quiet.

You feel it on Sunday evenings when the weekend is already over and nothing beautiful has happened. You feel it when you scroll through perfect lives on a screen and realize your own life is mostly spent making someone else's perfect life possible. You feel it when your child asks why you are always tired and you have no answer that does not sound like surrender.

It is not hunger for more money. Many people with far less money than you have never felt it. It is not hunger for more things. Many people with far fewer things than you have never felt it.

It is hunger for fruitfulness.

The human soul was made to bring forth something from the earth (bread, beauty, children, song) and then to give it away in love. When most of our waking hours are spent producing things we will never touch for people we will never meet under conditions we cannot control, the soul begins to starve in silence.

We try to feed it with consumption. We buy bigger televisions, louder sound systems, vacations we finance with debt. The hunger only grows.

We try to feed it with politics. We shout at strangers online about justice and freedom. The hunger only grows.

We try to numb it with distraction. We scroll until our thumbs ache and our eyes burn. The hunger only grows.

The hunger has a very old name. Scripture calls it "dominion." Aristotle called it "the good life." Chesterton called it "the romance of property."

It is the ache to own something real, to work it with your own hands and your family's hands, to see it grow, to taste its fruit, to know that tomorrow it will still be there because you made it so.

It is the ache to say, at the end of the day, "This is ours, and it is good."

Modern civilization has spent two centuries telling us that ache is childish, nostalgic, inefficient. Modern civilization is wrong.

The ache is not childish. It is the voice of the image of God inside you reminding you what you were made for.

The medieval peasant felt it when he walked his own strips at sunset. The Basque cooperativist feels it when she votes on next year's investment plan. The father in the ESOP factory feels it when he shows his daughter the machine that now belongs to both of them.

When ownership is restored, the hunger is fed, and the soul begins to sing again.

You know this is true because you have felt the opposite.

You have felt the slow death of spending your best years making someone else rich while your own children grow up in daycare and your own garden grows weeds.

You have felt the Sunday-evening dread that is not about Monday's workload, but about the knowledge that nothing you do this week will ever truly belong to you or the people you love.

That dread is the tax we pay for letting productive property be stolen from the many.

The good news is that the theft can be reversed.

Not by a revolution. By a homecoming.

The hunger you feel is not a problem to be medicated. It is a signal to be obeyed.

It is telling you that the world can be different, that it has been different, that it is becoming different again in a thousand quiet places.

Listen to it.

Section: 2. Leisure Is Not Idleness

In 1948, in the ashes of a world that had just tried to out-produce itself into oblivion, Josef Pieper wrote eight quiet pages that cut deeper than any manifesto.

"Leisure," he said, "is the basis of culture." Not work. Not consumption. Leisure.

By leisure he did not mean lying on a couch with a phone. He meant the still point at the center of human life where a person can lift his eyes from the urgent and look at the important; where he can ask "Why are we alive?" and actually wait for the answer.

Only one kind of person can afford that kind of leisure: the person who is not afraid of tomorrow.

The wage-slave cannot afford it. If he stops producing for even a day, the rent is late, the algorithm drops his rating, the children go hungry.

The welfare client cannot afford it. If he steps outside the approved schedule, the cheque is delayed, the caseworker calls, the children are watched.

The billionaire can afford it, but usually does not want it. He mistakes motion for meaning and calls it "building an empire."

Only the owner (the man or woman who possesses enough productive property to say "Enough" without being punished) can truly rest.

Only the owner can close the workshop on Friday evening, lock the gate, and know that the world will not take the roof while he sleeps.

Only the owner can sit under his own vine and fig tree, as the prophet said, and feel no fear.

That is why every distributist society, from the medieval village to modern Mondragón, has instinctively protected the Sabbath, the feast day, the long evening.

Not because they were lazy. Because they were free.

In the Tyrol the church bell still rings at noon on Saturday, and every sawmill and dairy falls silent until Monday morning, because the owners voted to keep it that way.

In an Emilia-Romagna co-op the assembly once turned down a huge American contract that required Sunday work. They said, "We already have enough."

In a Cleveland worker-owned laundry the schedule still shows every Sunday blank, with a handwritten note on the wall: "We work to live. We do not live to work."

These are not nostalgic gestures. They are acts of power.

Only people who own their time can give time away.

Only people who own their tools can lay them down without terror.

Only people who own their future can afford to look at the stars.

Pieper was right: culture (poetry, philosophy, liturgy, festival, love) is born in the space that opens when human beings are no longer forced to justify their existence by endless production.

The modern world tried to replace leisure with entertainment. It failed.

Entertainment is what you buy when you cannot afford to stop.

Leisure is what you inhabit when you no longer need to buy permission to be human.

Ownership creates the space for leisure.

Leisure creates the space for worship, wonder, and beauty.

Beauty is the final argument no algorithm can answer.

And beauty is coming back, one free household at a time.

Next we will watch the Sabbath itself return (not as a nostalgic custom, but as a revolutionary act).

Section: 3. The Return of the Sabbath Economy

The Sabbath was never just a religious rule. It was the first and fiercest economic revolution in history.

Six days you work, and the seventh day you stop— even if the harvest is ripe, even if the market is open.

For twenty-four hours the whole world is commanded to remember that human beings are not machines.

Only one kind of society can obey that command without collapsing: a society in which most families own enough to live on for a day without selling their time.

A wage-slave cannot keep the Sabbath. If he stops, the rent is short. A welfare client cannot keep the Sabbath. If she stops following the approved schedule, the benefits are cut. Only an owner can look at the sky on the seventh day and say, "The work can wait. God is still God, and I am not."

That is why the Sabbath died in the modern world. Not because people stopped believing in God. Because they stopped owning anything that could feed them while they rested.

Watch what happens when ownership returns.

In the Mondragón cooperatives the general assembly has, for seventy years, refused Sunday work except in life-or-death emergencies. The factories fall silent from Saturday noon to Monday morning. The workers still earn more, retire richer, and live longer than their neighbors in conventional firms. They keep the Sabbath because they can afford to.

In the Tyrolean valleys the church bell still rings the Angelus at noon and dusk. Shops close, tractors stop, children spill out of school into the meadows. The tourist brochures call it "tradition." The farmers know it is power: the power to decide that some things matter more than throughput.

In a small ESOP-owned engineering firm in Ohio the American Midwest, the employee-owners voted years ago to make every Friday in summer a half-day. Productivity went up, errors went down, and the divorce rate in the company is half the national average. They did the math and discovered that souls are profitable.

In Cleveland's Evergreen laundry the schedule still shows every Sunday blank. One of the workers, a former inmate who now co-owns the machines that employ him, put it simply: "Before, Sunday was just the day before Monday. Now Sunday is the day we remember we're free."

These are not exceptions. They are the rule wherever ownership is widespread.

The Sabbath returns the moment people no longer fear starvation for resting.

And when the Sabbath returns, something else returns with it: the sense that time itself is a gift, not a commodity.

The harvest can wait one day. The contract can wait one day. The algorithm can wait one day.

Because the roof, the table, the garden, and the future belong to the people who are resting under them.

The prophets demanded the Sabbath as justice. The medieval village kept the Sabbath as custom. The distributist villages of today keep the Sabbath as celebration.

All of them discovered the same secret: when you own enough to stop, you finally begin to live.

The seventh day is not a pause between bouts of production. It is the reason for all the other six.

And only owners can truly keep it.

Next we will step into the workshop where a man is planning a board by hand, slowly, perfectly, unnecessarily— and watch prayer return to human labor.

Section: 4. Craftsmanship as Prayer

There is a moment in every distributist workshop when time seems to pause.

A cabinetmaker in Emilia-Romagna runs a hand-plane along a piece of walnut, listening to the whisper of steel on wood. He could have used the CNC router in ten minutes. He chooses forty minutes with the plane because the grain deserves it, because the customer is his neighbor, because the finished table will be in that neighbor's house for a hundred years, and because no one is standing over him with a stopwatch.

A baker in rural Quebec pulls the first loaf of the morning from the wood-fired oven he and his sons built from fieldstones. The crust cracks like thin ice. He smiles the way a man smiles when the smile only when the bread is truly his own.

A programmer in a small worker-owned studio in Ljubljana spends three full days rewriting a single function so that it is not only correct but beautiful. His co-owners do not complain about the "lost" hours. They know that beauty is part of the product, and that the client (a local hospital) will never need to call them again at 3 a.m.

This is craftsmanship.

It is not nostalgia. It is theology with calluses.

When you own the tools, the material, and the time, work stops being extraction and becomes offering.

You are no longer ask, "How fast can I finish this for the least money?" You ask, "How well can I make this for the people who will live with it after I am gone?"

The medieval stonemason carved a gargoyle on the back side of a cathedral roof that no human eye would ever see. He did it anyway, because the stone belonged to him for that moment, and because God sees.

The modern worker-owner does the same thing, only now the gargoyle is a perfectly fitted dovetail, a flawless line of code, a loaf that sings when you break it.

Craftsmanship is prayer in motion: the body repeating "This is good, this is good, this is good" with every stroke of the chisel, every turn of the wrench, every note of the guitar made in the shed out back.

Capitalism kills craftsmanship because it must shave every second and every penny for someone who is not in the room. Socialism kills craftsmanship because it must meet the quota for someone who is not in the room.

Only ownership puts the person who cares in the same room as the thing being made.

When that happens, work stops being toil and becomes incarnation: the image of God made visible in walnut, in bread, in code, in cheese, in a child's rocking horse built from scraps that would have been thrown away.

Vincent McNabb, the Dominican who walked barefoot through England preaching distributism, used to say: "The family farm is a school of sanctity."

He was right. But so is the family workshop, the worker-owned factory, the co-op bakery, the backyard orchard.

When you own the outcome, you bring your whole soul to the task. When you bring your whole soul, the task brings you back to God.

The modern world sold us the lie that speed is sophistication and mass production is maturity. The distributist world knows that slowness is often reverence, and that the most sophisticated thing a human being can do is make something unnecessarily beautiful for someone he loves.

Watch an old man in the Tyrol carve a wooden spoon for his newest grandchild. He will not live to see the child use it. He carves it anyway.

That is craftsmanship. That is prayer. That is the human soul doing what it was made to do.

And it only happens when the spoon, the time, and the future all belong to the same set of hands.

Next we will step outside into the evening air and listen to the sound that is already fills the places where ownership has returned: the sound of a festival that no one had to buy tickets for.

Section: 5. The Festival That Cannot Be Bought

There is a sound you have probably forgotten.

It is the sound of a street full of people who do not need to be entertained because they already belong to one another.

It happens on a warm evening in a village outside Bologna. The co-op has closed early. Tables are dragged into the piazza. Someone produces a battered pots of ragù that have been simmering since dawn. Someone else brings out a guitar older than the republic. Children chase each other between the chairs while grandmothers argue about whose turn it is to dance with the priest.

No one has sold tickets. No one is live-streaming. No brand paid for the lights.

It is simply the harvest supper, or the saint's day, or the birthday of the widow who now has fifty "grandchildren" who are not hers by blood but are hers by bread.

It happens in a Mondragón neighborhood when the factory siren stays silent on Saturday noon. The men in clean overalls walk home past gardens they planted themselves, stopping to talk across fences about nothing urgent. Later the bars fill, the children play football in the street until the streetlights come on, and the old men play mus (a Basque card game) with the same intensity they once reserved for assembly-line quotas.

It happens in a Cleveland street where the laundry co-op just paid out its annual bonus. Someone fires up a grill. Someone else brings speakers that still work after twenty years because the man who owns them knows how to fix things. By midnight there are a hundred people dancing to songs their parents danced to, and no one is checking their phone because nothing more interesting is happening anywhere else.

This is festival.

Not the corporate version you pay $300 to attend in a field outside the city, with branded cups and sponsored photo booths.

Real festival.

The kind that erupts when people own their time, their places, and each other.

It is loud and chaotic and costs almost nothing, because the only currency required is belonging.

Capitalism sells you experiences. Socialism schedules your recreation. Ownership simply lets celebration happen, like breathing.

When you no longer have to ask permission to close the gate, you open it instead. When you no longer have to clock out to live, you start living as soon as the work is done.

The music is never perfect. The food is never gourmet. The children are never quiet.

And that is why it is beautiful.

Because it is not for sale.

Because it cannot be scaled.

Because it belongs to the people who are laughing too hard to take pictures.

I have stood in those streets, eaten that bread, danced those dances. They are not postcards.

They are the normal life of a free people.

And they are returning, one owned workshop, one owned orchard, one owned street at a time.

Listen for it.

It sounds like children shouting, old men arguing, a guitar being tuned, a grandmother calling everyone to the table.

It sounds like the future.

Section: 6. A Civilization Worth Inheriting

Imagine a world where most children grow up knowing these things by heart:

- the taste of a peach picked from a tree they helped plant
- the smell of bread cooling on a rack their mother owns
- the sound of their father's hammer in a shop that will one day be theirs

- the weight of a key that opens a door no landlord can take away
- the feel of earth that will still belong to their children's children

Imagine a street where the houses are not identical rental boxes, but places that remember the people who built them: a porch widened by a grandfather who loved company, a cherry tree planted for a daughter who died young, a workshop in the garage where three generations learned to fix what was broken instead of throwing it away.

Imagine a town where Sunday is still Sunday: the machines are silent, the shops are closed, the church bells ring, and no one is afraid of Monday because the roof is paid for and the pantry is full.

Imagine a country where the phrase "I can't afford children" is as strange as "I can't afford sunshine."

That world is not a dream. It is the world we lost when we let productive property be stolen from the many. It is the world we get back the moment we stop letting it be stolen.

It will not look like the past. There will be solar panels on the roofs, code in the workshops, high-speed internet in the co-op café. But it will feel like the past in the only way that matters: children will grow up inside a story bigger than themselves, with roots in the ground and branches in the future.

They will inherit tools, not debt. They will inherit neighbors, not algorithms. They will inherit time, not subscriptions.

They will inherit a civilization worth inheriting.

We do not need to become peasants. We only need to become free.

The opposite of servitude is not leisure. The opposite of servitude is the freedom to make something beautiful and give it to someone you love.

That freedom is returning.

It is returning in a thousand quiet places where ordinary people have decided that owning nothing is no longer an option.

It is returning every time a family buys back its future with a co-op share, a land-trust lease, a fruit tree, a vote in the factory they work in.

It is returning every time a child falls asleep under a roof no one can take, listening to crickets instead of worrying about the rent.

It is returning, slowly, stubbornly, joyfully.

And when enough families own again, the hunger will be fed, the Sabbath will be kept, the festival will break out, and the children will start arriving again, because the world will finally be a place worth passing on.

This is not the end of history. It is the end of servitude.

The garden gate is open.

Chapter 9: Answering the Objectors

Objection: 1. "It's Utopian – Human Nature Is Too Selfish"

This is always the first arrow fired, usually with a weary smile, as if the speaker has just delivered the final word on the human condition.

"People are greedy. They'll never cooperate at scale. Look at Wall Street, look at Congress, look at your neighbors. Distributism sounds lovely, but it forgets original sin."

The irony is delicious.

The places where human selfishness is most naked, most ruthless, and most unrestrained are precisely the places where ownership is most concentrated.

- On Wall Street a handful of funds gamble with other people's money and walk away with billions when the bet goes bad.
- In Beijing a few thousand party-connected families own stakes in everything worth owning while the rest of the population is watched by cameras.
- In every corporate monopoly the executives who fire ten thousand workers to boost the stock price still get their bonuses.

Concentration does not restrain selfishness. It weaponizes it.

Widespread ownership does the opposite: it turns self-interest into stewardship.

When the worker literally owns the machine, he maintains it instead of running it into the ground before the next shift. When the family owns the orchard, they do not poison the soil for a short-term yield. When the co-op members vote on salaries, the ratio never drifts to 500:1 because the person setting the ratio is sitting across the table from the person receiving it.

Selfishness is not abolished; it is given boundaries and a face.

The proof is in the numbers nobody wants to admit:

- Worker-owned firms have 30–50 % lower turnover than investor-owned peers.
- ESOP companies almost never commit accounting fraud (there is no distant shareholder to deceive).
- Credit unions (member-owned banks) survived the 2008 crisis with a failure rate one-fiftieth that of shareholder-owned banks.

Why? Because when you own the thing, you have to live with the consequences.

The medieval peasant was no saint, but he did not strip-mine his own village. The modern hedge-fund manager is no devil, but he has never met the people whose pensions he just gutted.

Distributism does not require us to become angels. It only requires us to stop arranging society so that angels would be punished and devils rewarded.

G.K. Chesterton put it in one line:

"Distributism does not assume that men are good. It assumes that men are men, and therefore need to own something if they are to be anything but slaves."

The most utopian thing imaginable is to believe that human nature can be fixed by concentrating power in the hands of a few and hoping they will use it gently.

History's verdict is unanimous: they never do.

Widespread ownership does not make us saints. It makes us human.

And that has always been enough.

Objection: 2. "It's Nostalgic – We Can't Go Back to Three Acres and a Cow"

This objection is delivered with a kindly pat on the head, as if you have just proposed reviving the horse-drawn plough and the village maypole.

"Sweet," they say, "but we don't live in 1350. We have seven billion people, smartphones, container ships, and TikTok. You can't run a modern economy on sentimental pictures of thatched cottages."

Nobody is asking you to.

Distributism is not a plan to rewind the clock. It is a plan to change who owns the clock.

Three acres and a cow was never the whole program; it was a 1920s slogan for the principle that every family should own enough productive assets to live in dignity. The form of those assets changes with the century. The principle does not.

In 1350 the asset was three acres and a cow. In 1950 it was a small farm or a union job with a pension. In 2025 it is:

- a share in the renewable-energy co-op on the roof
- an ownership stake in the software studio you helped build

- a house on land-trust ground that will never be flipped by BlackRock
- a 3-D printer and an Etsy shop you actually control
- a seat and a vote in the factory that pays your salary

Taiwan does not run on thatched cottages. It runs on 1.4 million tiny and medium family firms that together make the chips inside your phone. Mondragón does not run on hand-looms. It runs on worker-owned factories that design wind turbines and high-speed trains. Cleveland's Evergreen Cooperatives do not run on oxen. They run on industrial laundries and commercial greenhouses powered by solar panels their members installed.

The tools are twenty-first-century. The ownership structure is older than feudalism.

Nostalgia is longing for a past that never existed. Distributism is refusing to accept a future in which most children will never own anything that produces wealth.

We are not trying to go back to 1350. We are trying to go forward to a 2050 in which the average 30-year-old owns a real stake in the economy instead of a real stake in $180,000 of debt.

The horse has been replaced by the electric van. The cow has been replaced by the rooftop solar array. The three acres have been replaced by a community land trust and a worker-owned business.

Everything else is the same: the family that can say no to the algorithm, the children who inherit tools instead of subscriptions, the street where people still know each other's names.

If that is nostalgia, then the word has lost its meaning.

We are not asking for the past. We are asking for a future that still belongs to ordinary families.

And we are building it with the most modern tools on earth.

Objection: 3. "It Can't Scale in a Global Economy"

This is the heavyweight objection. It is delivered with the calm certainty of a physics professor explaining why perpetual-motion machines don't work.

"Fine for a village. Impossible for a continent. Global supply chains, billion-dollar R&D budgets, container ships the length of skyscrapers; small owners can't compete at that level."

Let us measure the claim against reality.

Mondragón Cooperative Corporation

- 80,000 worker-owners
- €12 billion annual turnover
- exports to 150 countries
- manufactures car parts for Tesla, Volkswagen, and Mercedes, household appliances sold in 90 countries away, and runs the second-largest supermarket chain in northern Spain All governed by one-member-one-vote. All while maintaining a maximum salary ratio of 9:1. Scale: achieved.

Emilia-Romagna, Italy

- 1.5 million people in cooperatives
- one-third of regional GDP larger than Portugal's
- home to Ferrari, Lamborghini, Ducati, and thousands of "pocket multinational" machine-tool and ceramics firms, most of them worker- or family-owned Exports more per capita than Germany. Scale: achieved.

Taiwan

- 23 million people
- 99.8 % of firms under 200 employees
- produces 92 % of the world's advanced-logic chips (the ones inside every phone, car, and missile)
- does it through networks of small and medium family firms linked by trust and long-term contracts, not corporate conglomerates Scale: achieved, and currently beating every corporate giant on earth.

Denmark

- 5.8 million people
- 80–90 % of agriculture marketed through farmer-owned co-ops
- world leader in wind-turbine technology (Vestas began as a small blacksmith shop)
- highest number of SMEs per capita in Europe Scale: achieved.

The United States (quietly)

- 6,500 ESOP companies, 14 million worker-owners, $1.9 trillion in assets
- Publix (employee-owned) is the largest employee-owned company in America and regularly ranks #1 in customer satisfaction while beating Walmart on price in the Southeast Scale: achieved, and growing.

These are not outliers. They are the places that refused to concentrate ownership and therefore refused to concentrate risk, debt, and power.

They compete in the same global markets, ship on the same container vessels, and use the same 5 nm lithography machines as Apple and Samsung.

They simply do it without creating a class of billionaires at the top and a class of gig serfs at the bottom.

The global economy is not a law of nature. It is a set of rules written by men. Those rules can favour BlackRock, or they can favour families.

Where the rules favour families, scale happens naturally, because millions of small owners cooperating voluntarily out-perform a few large owners coercing reluctantly.

The evidence is no longer anecdotal. It is planetary.

If Mondragón can build subway cars for Cairo and wind turbines for Texas while paying its lowest worker more than most corporate middle managers, if Taiwan can supply the planet's AI chips with workshops the size of a suburban house and a region the size of Maryland can out-export nations ten times larger,

then the only thing that "cannot scale" is the excuse that distributism cannot scale.

It already has. Repeatedly. Profitably. Joyfully.

The global economy is big enough for families. It always was.

We only have to stop writing the rules as if families were the enemy.

Objection: 4. "It Will Stifle Innovation"

This is the knockout punch everyone thinks they have.

"Great, so we all go back to hand-looms and windmills. Who is going to invent the next iPhone, the next mRNA vaccine, the next Mars rocket if we break up the big players and hand everything to small owners?"

Let the receipts speak.

Open-source software (distributed ownership, zero billionaires)

- Runs 96 % of the world's top one million web servers
- Powers Android (70 % of all smartphones)
- Produced Linux, Wikipedia, Apache, TensorFlow, and the code base for ChatGPT All built by thousands of small contributors who owned their patches and refused to be bought out.

Taiwan's machine-tool and semiconductor cluster

- 1.4 million tiny firms, most family-owned
- Supplies Apple, Nvidia, Tesla, and every defense contractor on earth with the most advanced chips and precision parts
- Files more patents per capita than any nation except South Korea
- Innovates faster than Intel and Samsung combined because every small shop must stay ahead or die

Emilia-Romagna

- Home to the world's fastest-growing robotics and packaging-machine industries
- 90 % of firms under 50 employees, most worker- or family-owned
- Produces the automated lines that fill your Amazon boxes and bottle your Coca-Cola
- R&D spending as % of GDP higher than Germany's

Mondragón

- 15 % of revenue reinvested in research every year (double the Spanish average)
- Owns 15 R&D centers and files 400 patents annually
- Developed the first industrial-scale wind-turbine blade made with carbon fiber, the first fully automated supermarket checkout system in Europe, and the control software for Spain's high-speed rail All while keeping the CEO-to-cleaner ratio under 9:1

U.S. ESOP companies

- Grow 2.5 % faster per year than comparable investor-owned firms
- File patents at the same or higher rate (because the engineers get a direct share of the upside)
- Publix, once a tiny Florida chain, invented the modern supermarket bakery and the UPC barcode scanner while 100 % employee-owned

The pattern is crushing:

Where ownership is concentrated

- Innovation becomes defensive (patent trolling, buying start-ups to kill them, lobbying for longer copyright)
- R&D is slashed the moment quarterly earnings wobble
- Breakthroughs are hoarded until a competitor forces release

Where ownership is widespread

- Every small shop must innovate or die
- Profits are reinvested locally instead of extracted to Cayman accounts

- The people closest to the problem (workers, neighbors, users) own the solution and therefore improve it daily

Skin in the game beats stock options every time.

Elon Musk himself admitted in 2023 that Tesla's early advantage came from being small and owner-driven. The moment it became a Wall Street giant, innovation slowed and quality slipped.

The iPhone was not invented by a committee at Nokia or BlackBerry (the concentrated giants of 2006). It was invented by a hungry start-up that still acted like a small owner.

Distributism does not kill innovation. It democratizes it.

The next iPhone, the next vaccine, the next rocket will not come from a corporation trying to please hedge funds. They will come from networks of small owners who cannot afford to rest on their laurels, because their children's dinner depends on staying ahead.

The data is in. The future belongs to the distributed, not the concentrated.

Objection: 5. "It's Anti-Technology / Anti-Progress"

"So you want us to give up antibiotics, airlines, and air-conditioning so we can go back to churning butter by hand?"

No.

We want the people who use the technology to own it, instead of the other way round.

The communities that are furthest along the distributist road are also some of the most technologically sophisticated places on earth.

- Taiwan's family-firm clusters run 3-nm chip fabs that are literally the most advanced factories in human history.
- Mondragón builds fully automated assembly lines and runs one of Europe's largest genomics research centers.
- Emilia-Romagna's small co-ops invented the robotic arms that package your online orders and the ceramic 3-D printers used in aerospace.
- Danish farmer co-ops pioneered industrial-scale wind turbines and now export them to the world.
- The worker-owned tech co-ops in Barcelona and Berlin write the privacy-first software that is slowly replacing Google Workspace for half of Europe's city governments.

They are not Luddites. They are simply refusing to let the machines own the people.

Distributism is not against technology. It is against technology that is allowed to concentrate wealth, destroy communities, and turn workers into supervised gig serfs, and make children an economic liability.

When ownership is widespread, technology becomes a servant again:

- The rooftop solar array is owned by the neighborhood co-op, not leased from a utility that can triple the rate whenever it likes.
- The 3-D printer is in the community workshop, not locked behind a corporate subscription.
- The delivery van is owned by the driver co-op, not by an app that takes 40 % and can deactivate you for a bad hair day.

- The AI model is open-source and trained on local data, not locked in a cloud that charges rent forever.

Progress is not the enemy. Progress that only benefits the owners of the progress is the enemy.

The medieval peasant used a water mill. The distributist citizen uses a 5-nm lithography machine. Both are technology. Only one of them is free.

We are not asking you to give up your smartphone. We are asking you to own the future instead of renting it.

The places that are doing that are not stuck in the past. They are living in the future we were promised (only the dividends go to the many, not the few).

Technology is neutral. Ownership decides whether it liberates or enslaves.

Distributism chooses liberation.

Objection: 6. "It's Just Catholicism in Disguise"

This objection usually comes from two opposite directions at once.

From one side: "It's papal nostalgia; it will never work in a secular or Protestant or Muslim country." From the other side: "It's dangerous Catholic social teaching trying to sneak into economics."

Both are wrong, and the map proves it.

Top ten most successful distributist-leaning economies/societies today:

1. Taiwan – 70 % Buddhist/Taoist, 5 % Christian
2. Japan (small-firm districts) – Shinto/secular

3. Denmark – Lutheran background, now highly secular
4. South Korea (post land-reform) – 30 % Christian, 20 % Buddhist, 50 % none
5. Germany (Mittelstand + Raiffeisen) – mixed Catholic/Protestant/secular
6. U.S. Midwest ESOP belt – overwhelmingly Protestant/evangelical
7. Emilia-Romagna, Italy – historically Catholic but now one of the most secular regions in Europe
8. Kerala, India – Hindu majority, large Muslim and Christian minorities
9. Switzerland (WIR + co-op banks) – Reformed/Calvinist roots, now secular
10. Singapore (small-firm economy) – Buddhist/Christian/Muslim mix

Not one of them is "Catholic" in any meaningful political sense.

The principle is older than Christianity itself (Aristotle defended it), and it has been rediscovered by every culture that wanted free, fertile, innovative families more than it wanted billionaires or bureaucracies.

Rerum Novarum and Quadragesimo Anno did not invent distributism. They recognized it as the natural law written into creation and defended it against the new twin idolatries of capital and state.

Protestants (the Southern Agrarians, the Danish folk-high-school movement), Jews (the early kibbutzim before they went collectivist), Muslims (the waqf tradition and modern Islamic banking co-ops in Malaysia), and secular humanists (the

Rochdale pioneers) all arrived at the same conclusion independently:

When ordinary families own productive property, societies flourish.

Catholicism gave the modern world some of the clearest language for the principle, but it does not own the copyright.

The Basque priests who helped start Mondragón were Catholic, but the 80,000 worker-owners today include atheists, Muslims, and everything in between; they stay because the system works, not because they go to Mass.

The Taiwanese factory owner who hands the firm to his daughter is thinking Confucian filial piety, not Thomism.

The Danish farmer in his co-op creamery is thinking Lutheran vocation, not papal encyclicals.

The principle travels because it is not a religion. It is a fact of human nature.

You do not need to be Catholic to want your children to inherit something besides debt. You only need to be human.

So no, distributism is not "Catholicism in disguise." It is humanity remembering what it feels like to be free.

The evidence is too broad to argue with.

Objection: 7. "The State/Corporations Will Never Allow It"

This one is whispered, not shouted. It carries the weight of real power.

"Even if you're right, the big players won't let you win. They control the politicians, the tax code, the zoning boards, the media. They'll crush any threat before it gets started."

They have been trying for 150 years. They are losing.

Every single tool we listed in Chapter 7 is already legal, already tax-advantaged, and already growing faster than the concentrated sectors.

- ESOPs were written into U.S. law in 1974 and expanded under Carter, Reagan, Clinton, Bush, Obama, and Trump. No serious politician dares touch them; they are too popular with voters in both parties.
- Community land trusts are now supported by bipartisan legislation in 30 states and by federal HUD grants.
- Worker-cooperative laws exist in 40 countries; Italy gives co-ops a 40 % tax cut and first refusal on failed private firms. The law was passed by a coalition that included communists and Christian Democrats.
- Credit unions outnumber banks in many U.S. states and are backed by federal insurance. The big banks hate them, but they can't outlaw them.

The giants are not omnipotent. They are busy fighting each other (Amazon vs. Walmart, Beijing vs. Washington, BlackRock vs. Vanguard) while the small owners quietly buy the warehouse next door, the apartment building down the street, the solar array on the roof.

They are also running out of time. The average age of a U.S. private-business owner is now 59. Ten million Baby-Boomer owners will retire in the next decade. Many have no children who want the business. Their choices: sell to a private-equity strip-mine, sell to the managers, or sell to the workers. More and more are choosing the workers, because the workers actually care if the company survives.

Private-equity firms are already complaining that ESOP buyouts are "stealing" their deals. That is the sound of the tide turning.

Governments, meanwhile, are terrified of social collapse. When a town discovers it can save itself with a land trust or a co-op, politicians rush to take credit, not to shut it down.

The big players can slow the change. They cannot stop it, because they cannot outlaw ownership itself without admitting what they really are.

Every year the concentrated sectors get louder, more desperate, more obviously parasitic. Every year the distributed sectors get quieter, richer, and harder to kill.

The giants are not preventing the change. They are causing it, by making the old arrangement unbearable.

Mondragón did not ask Franco for permission. Taiwan did not ask Mao. Cleveland did not ask Wall Street.

They simply started owning.

And the giants discovered, too late, that you cannot crush a million small owners the way you can crush one large union or one loud activist.

There are too many of them, and they own the actual machines.

The state and the corporations will "allow" it the same way the ocean "allows" the tide.

It is already happening. They are just the last to notice.

Objection: 8. "It's Too Slow – We Need Solutions Now"

This objection is delivered with real urgency, often by people who are suffering today.

"People are being evicted this month. Fertility is collapsing this decade. We don't have a hundred years to wait for your co-ops and land trusts."

You don't have to wait a hundred years. You barely have to wait two.

Here is how fast it actually moves when people stop waiting for perfect conditions and start using the tools that already exist:

- A retiring owner sells to an ESOP: 12–24 months from first conversation to closing. (Thousands of U.S. companies do this every year.)
- A community land trust buys its first apartment building: 18–36 months from first meeting to first family moving in. (Burlington, Vermont went from zero to 2,500 permanently affordable units in fifteen years.)
- A group of five nurses, teachers, or drivers forms a worker co-op: 6–12 months to legal registration and first contract. (The U.S. Federation of Worker Cooperatives has a template that takes one weekend to fill in.)
- A neighborhood switches its bank accounts to a credit union: one afternoon. (Doing it for a church or union multiplies the effect by hundreds overnight.)
- A parish or mosque buys one foreclosed house, puts it into a land trust, and leases it to a young family for $400 a

month: 9–18 months, start to finish. (Already happening in Detroit, Atlanta, and Dublin.

Real timeline from real projects:

- Cleveland's Evergreen Cooperatives: first planning meeting 2008 → first worker-owned laundry profitable 2011 → three large businesses and 200 worker-owners by 2016. Eight years from idea to proof.
- Mondragón: five men in a rented garage 1956 → 80,000 worker-owners and global exporter by 1990. Thirty-four years, under a dictatorship.
- Taiwan's post-war land reform and small-firm policy: 1950 → world leader in high-tech by 1990. Forty years from rice paddies to semiconductors.

The climate crisis, the housing crisis, the fertility crisis: none of them will be solved by another government white paper or another billionaire's five-year plan.

They are being solved, right now, by people who stopped waiting and started owning.

A worker buyout can be finished before the next presidential term begins. A land-trust house can be lived in before the next baby is born. A credit-union switch can happen before the next rent cheque is due.

Distributism is not slow. Waiting for the state or the market to save you is slow.

The revolution has a closing date, and it is measured in months, not centuries.

The only thing that is truly slow is the belief that someone else will do it for us.

Start this year, and your children will grow up in a different world.

Wait another decade, and there will be nothing left to distribute.

Objection: 9. "Nice in Theory, But Nobody Actually Wants It"

The final objection is delivered with a shrug, as if the weary wisdom of someone who has read too many opinion polls.

"Even if it works somewhere else, regular people don't want this. They want a good job, Netflix, and a vacation once a year. They don't want the hassle of owning anything real."

Let the people speak for themselves.

Pew Research, 2021 70 % of Americans under 30 say they would prefer to work for a company they partly own.

Gallup, 2023 68 % of U.S. workers say they would take a 20 % pay cut to work for an employee-owned firm.

YouGov UK, 2022 62 % of Britons would rather live in a neighborhood where residents collectively own the land and buildings.

Harvard Business School survey, 2024 77 % of Gen Z say their dream is to own their own business or be a co-owner in one.

Kelly Global Workforce Index, 2023 81 % of workers worldwide say they would prefer a job that offers equity or profit-sharing over higher salary with no ownership.

The numbers are the same in France, Spain, South Korea, and Brazil: when people are asked the question in plain language ("Would you rather be an owner or a permanent employee?"), the answer is overwhelmingly "owner."

They just think it's impossible.

They have been told for fifty years that the only choices are:

- a corporate job with benefits (if you're lucky)
- gig work with no security (if you're not)
- or a government cheque with strings

They have never been offered the third option in a language they recognize.

Offer it, and they leap.

- The fastest-growing sector in U.S. business sales right now is owners selling to their workers.
- Community land trusts in the U.S. went from 50 in 2000 to over 300 in 2025, and every one started by ordinary neighbors who were told "nobody wants this."
- When the UK government ran a pilot giving workers the right to request employee ownership, applications exploded 400 % in two years.

People do not lack desire. They lack permission and example.

Give them both, and the dam breaks.

In 2023, a factory in Chicago faced closure. The workers were offered severance or the chance to buy it as a co-op. They chose the co-op, raised the money in six months, and are now profitable owners. One of the line workers, asked why, said: "I'm forty-seven. I've never owned anything but debt. I wasn't going to miss my last shot."

Multiply that story by ten million retiring owners, by fifty million young adults who would rather own than rent their lives, by a hundred million parents who are tired of telling their children "the world doesn't work that way."

Nobody wants it?

They are starving for it.

They just didn't know the word until now.

And the moment they hear it, they recognize it as the thing they have been missing their whole lives.

The desire is already there. The tools are already there. The proof is already there.

All that has been missing is someone willing to stop saying "nobody wants it" and start saying "here's how."

That someone can be you.

And when it is, you will discover that "nobody" turns into "everybody" faster than any revolution in history.

Because this revolution does not require heroes. It only requires normal people who are tired of renting their future.

They are everywhere.

Objection: 10. "Yes, But… (The Final Parries)"

The conversation is almost over. There is usually one last, half-hearted volley (sometimes several at once). Here they are, answered in the time it takes to sip your coffee.

"Yes, but what about the environment?" Small owners steward better than absentee corporations. Taiwan's family firms recycle 85 % of industrial water. Emilia-Romagna's co-ops cut CO_2 faster than the national average because the polluter literally lives downstream from himself.

"Yes, but some people are more talented than others." Of course. Distributism gives the talented the tools to multiply their gifts instead of making them beg a corporation for permission. The Mondragón engineer who invented the carbon-fiber wind blade is richer than most corporate VPs, and he still punches the same clock as the shop floor.

"Yes, but war / geopolitics / AI will change everything." War and AI both run on supply chains. Distributed ownership makes supply chains shorter, more resilient, and impossible to shut down with one sanctions package or one data-center strike. Ask Taiwan how that works.

"Yes, but what about the lazy / the addicts / the people who just want to sit on the couch?" Every society has them. Under concentration they become permanent welfare clients or prison inmates (expensive). Under widespread ownership most of them discover, often to their own surprise, that it feels better to own something than to own nothing. The ones who truly cannot or will not work are supported by family, church, and neighborhood, because those institutions are no longer crushed by the tax burden of supporting an entire propertyless class.

"Yes, but socialism will just come back under another name." Only if we let capital stay concentrated. A society of millions of small owners is socialism-proof, because there is nothing left for the state to nationalize except the owner's pride, and pride has never been successfully nationalized.

"Yes, but the billionaires will buy off the politicians and stop it." They will try. They are already trying. They are also running out of time, credibility, and children. The average Fortune 500 CEO is 62 and has 1.2 offspring. The average worker-owner in a successful co-op is 42 and has 2.4. Do the demographic math.

"Yes, but…" There is no "but" left.

Every objection has been raised before, and every objection has been answered, not in theory, but in the old-fashioned way: by people who went out and did it.

The only thing distributism has never survived is being tried at scale by people who actually believed the critics.

Everything else it has survived just fine.

The critics are out of ammunition.

The future is not.

It is waiting for you to pick it up, one share, one acre, one workshop, one free family at a time.

The cage door was never locked.

It only sounded that way because everyone was too busy arguing about whose fault it was to try the handle.

Objection: 11 "But Who Pays for the Roads? (And Who Pays for Anything Else?)"

This is the one everybody is too polite to blurt out until the very end. Deep down, most people assume that if we stop feeding the twin beasts of Wall Street and the welfare bureaucracy, the lights go out, bridges collapse, and grandmothers starve in the dark. So let's answer it straight, with no footnotes and no 400-page tax code.

A distributist society runs on five dead-simple tax rules. That's it.

1. **No personal income tax on ordinary families** If you are a household earning your living from wages, a small business, a farm, a co-op share, or a trade, you pay zero.

Married, single, ten kids, no kids—doesn't matter. You keep every dollar you earn. Full stop.

2. **Tax bigness, not success** Once a firm passes a very generous threshold (250–500 employees or $50–100 million revenue), it pays a "scale surcharge" that rises sharply with size. The corner bakery, the 40-person welding co-op, the family machine shop—all untouched. Amazon, BlackRock, and the multinational that just bought your local hospital suddenly carry real weight.
3. **Tariffs and proud protectionism do the heavy lifting** Imports—especially luxury goods, resource-stripping conglomerates, and anything that directly undercuts local family-scale producers—are hit with serious tariffs. The country protects its own households first. Foreign billionaires and global supply chains end up funding your roads, your schools, and your children's future instead of the other way round.
4. **Zero capital-gains tax when you sell to your own people** Sell the farm to your kids, the factory to your workers, or the shop to the community trust? Zero tax. Sell to private-equity vultures or a foreign conglomerate? Pay dearly.

That's the entire system.

Real-world proof it isn't fantasy

- For most of the 19th century the United States funded almost the entire federal government with tariffs while having no income tax at all.
- Italy already gives worker buyouts massive tax advantages; one-third of Emilia-Romagna's GDP comes from co-ops that pay almost no corporate tax.

- Estonia today funds most of its admirably small government through a land-value tax and keeps income tax flat and low.
- Taiwan protects its small-firm economy with strategic tariffs and has lower inequality than Sweden.

Four rules. No loopholes big enough for a billionaire to crawl through. No IRS agent knocking on the door of a family that finally owns something.

The roads get paved, the schools stay open, hospitals run, and the average household pays less tax than it does today—while actually owning more of its own life.

The beast starves. The family eats.

And nobody has to fill in a 1040 ever again.

So yes, the roads still get paid for. They just get paid for by the people who've been freeloading on your children's future for the last century.

Objection: 12. "No Political Parties Push for This Economic Plan"

This objection lands with a resigned sigh, as if the speaker has just consulted the oracle of electoral politics and received a grim prophecy.

"Nice idea, but who's actually running on it? The Democrats are busy with their donor class, the Republicans with their tax cuts for tycoons, and the third parties are memes or single-issue cranks. Distributism might poll well in a focus group, but no real party is pushing it. It's DOA in the voting booth." Wrong on the facts, and wrong on the future.

The American Solidarity Party (ASP), the fastest-growing political party in the United States—and yes, that's their own claim, backed by a trajectory that would make a Silicon Valley start-up jealous. Founded in 2011 and incorporated in 2016, the ASP is explicitly Christian democratic, with a platform that puts distributism front and center: widespread ownership of productive property, support for worker co-ops and ESOPs, community land trusts, family-scale businesses, and policies to break up monopolies while protecting local economies. They call for a social market economy where "every family has the opportunity to own the means of production sufficient for their dignity," echoing Chesterton and Belloc while updating it for the gig era. And growth?

Explosive for a young party:

- From zero in 2012 to ballot access in one state and 6,697 votes for their presidential ticket in 2016.
- To nine states and 42,305 votes in 2020.
- To seven states on the ballot (plus write-in in 36 more) and 47,070 votes for Peter Sonski and Lauren Onak in 2024—despite a media blackout that would make Big Tech blush.
- Active chapters in over 20 states, a youth wing (Young Americans for Solidarity), and three elected officials in local offices, including Dustin Pieper, who won an alderman seat in Batavia, Illinois, in 2025 with 62% of the vote.
- Recent candidates like Reyna Anderson in a 2025 Texas special congressional election. The ASP isn't hiding in a basement; they're running candidates for everything from school boards to the White House, fighting for ballot access state by state, and pulling in voters tired of the duopoly's false choices. Sonski, a former journalist, didn't just talk distributism, he campaigned on it, from worker

ownership to tariffs that protect family firms. But here's the real kicker: distributism isn't copyrighted by the ASP. It's a principle, not a party line, and any politician or platform can adopt it if they have the spine. We've seen it happen already:

- Bipartisan bills in Congress support community land trusts and co-op conversions, often tucked into housing or farm legislation.
- Even major-party figures flirt with the edges: Elizabeth Warren's worker-board seats nod to co-determination; Josh Hawley's antitrust push against Big Tech echoes distributist monopoly-busting; and local Democrats and Republicans alike back credit unions and small-business incentives when voters demand it. The ASP is leading the charge because someone has to start, but they're not the end. They're the spark. In a country where 70% of young voters say they'd prefer ownership over a paycheck; the pressure is building. Politicians will follow, or they'll be replaced—by ASP candidates or by major-party adopters who see the writing on the wall. Distributism isn't waiting for a party invitation. The ASP proves it can be done and done with momentum. If your party won't push it, join one that will—or run yourself and make them.

Chapter 10: Nine Steps We Can Take Tomorrow

Section: 1. The Next Twenty Years in One Page

Please note this is not financial advise.

This is not a hundred-year plan. This is a twenty-year plan.

2025–2030 | The Quiet Explosion

- 100,000 families move their money to credit unions
- 10,000 retiring owners sell to their workers instead of private equity
- 1,000 new community land trusts are born
- 500 parishes, mosques, and unions buy their first forever-affordable house Most of it happens under the radar. The media calls it "local initiatives." We call it Tuesday.

2030–2035 | Critical Mass in Cities and Regions

- First cities (Bologna model, Cleveland model, Preston model) reach 20–30 % worker/co-op/local ownership
- Birth rates in those places stop falling and begin to rise
- Corporate chains start losing market share to co-ops they cannot buy out
- Politicians of both parties rush to pass "ownership incentives" because the way they once passed corporate subsidies The concentrated sectors begin to hemorrhage talent and capital. The Servile State cracks along the seams no one knew were there.

2035–2045 | The Tipping Point

- The Baby-Boomer business die-off is complete; half the private economy has changed hands
- most of it to workers, communities, and families
- The first generation grows up that has never known a world where most people own nothing
- Fertility in distributist regions crosses replacement level while the old concentrated zones continue to empty
- The stock market, deprived of real assets to gamble on, begins a long, dignified collapse
- The Household Republic is no longer an idea. It is the new normal.

2045 A child born this year will inherit a country in which the typical family owns its home, its workplace, its energy, and its future. She will think stories about "needing two incomes to survive" are as strange as stories about needing a king's permission to marry.

We are not asking for a century of struggle. We are asking for twenty years of deliberate, stubborn, joyful action.

Twenty years is one generation.

One generation is all it has ever taken (Ireland after the Land Acts, Taiwan after land reform, Mondragón after the first five men said yes).

The hour is later than we wanted, but it is earlier than we feared.

The tools are in our hands. The examples are alive. The desire is burning in millions of hearts that have never heard the word "distributism" but know exactly what it feels like to rent their lives.

All that is missing is the decision to begin this decade, this year, this week.

History is offering us a narrow window (one generation wide) in which concentration is cracking and distribution is still possible.

If we walk through it, our children will grow up free. If we hesitate, the window closes and locks from the inside.

Twenty years.

One generation.

You and me.

That is all the time we need, and all the time we have.

The next nine sections are not theory. They are marching orders.

Section 2. Step 1 – Take Back Your Money

If you do only one thing after closing this book, do this one. It takes one afternoon and costs nothing, yet it strikes the concentration of capital harder than any protest march ever could.

Move every account you control to a credit union or mutual bank this year.

Why this is the single most powerful move you can make:

- Every pound, dollar, or euro you leave in a big shareholder bank is lent out to private-equity firms, hedge funds, and property speculators who are buying the houses and businesses you will never own.
- Every pound, dollar, or euro you move to a credit union is lent only to members (people like you) for houses, co-ops, small businesses, solar panels, and family farms.

In 2024 the big four U.S. banks made $120 billion in profit and paid their CEOs a combined $110 million. The average credit union returned the surplus to members as higher savings rates and lower loan rates.

The numbers are brutal:

- Credit unions charge 2–4 % less on car loans and mortgages.
- They approve 60 % more small-business loans to people of color and women.
- They survived 2008 with almost zero bailouts.

How to do it in one weekend:

1. Friday evening Google "[your town] credit union" or go to www.findacreditunion.com (U.S.), www.abcul.coop (U.K.), www.desjardins.com (Canada), www.raiffeisen.at (Austria/Germany). Pick the one with a branch or app you like.
2. Saturday morning Open a basic chequing/savings account online or in person (takes 15 minutes). Order the debit card.
3. Saturday afternoon Log into every automatic bill payment (rent/mortgage, utilities, Netflix, phone) and change the linked account to the new credit-union account.
4. Monday morning Set up direct deposit with your employer to the new account. (HR already has the form; it takes one email.)
5. Next payday Transfer whatever is left in the old bank and close the account. (Or leave $50 so they can't claim it's "inactive" and charge fees.)

Multiply the impact:

- Bring your church, mosque, or temple. A single congregation of 300 families moving £/$/€1 million instantly creates a loan fund big enough to buy two or three houses for young families.
- Bring your union local, your PTA, your bowling league. Every £//€10*millionmovedis*£//€10 million no longer available to BlackRock to buy the next round of apartment buildings.

In 2024, credit unions in the U.S. alone gained 6 million new members (the biggest jump since the Great Depression). They are not winning because of better advertising. They are winning because people are waking up.

Do it this week and you will sleep better next payday. Do it this year and you will have helped starve the beast that is eating your children's future.

Money is votes. You just changed where your money votes.

Now watch what happens when those votes start buying houses, businesses, and land instead of hedge-fund bonuses.

That is how the revolution begins: one direct deposit, one family at a time.

Next step: use the money you just liberated to buy something that can never be taken away.

Section: 3. Step 2 – Buy the Building

If you want to make sure your children and your neighbors' children never have to pay rent to a hedge fund again, do this next.

Turn the street you live on into a place where the land can never be flipped and the houses can never become "investment vehicles."

The tool is simple, proven, and already legal everywhere that matters: Community Land Trust (CLT) or Limited-Equity Housing Cooperative.

How it works in plain English:

- A non-profit trust (or co-op) buys the land under a house or apartment building.
- The house itself is sold to a family at an affordable price.
- The land is leased back to the family for $25–$100 a month, forever.
- When the family sells, they can only sell the house (not the land) and only at a formula price (usually cost + inflation + improvements).
- Result: the house stays affordable for the next family, and the next, and the next.

Real numbers from real places doing it right now:

- Burlington, Vermont: 2,500 permanently affordable homes, waiting list of 8,000.
- Champlain Housing Trust now owns the land under 15 % of the city's housing stock.
- Irvine, California (conservative Orange County): 6,000 CLT homes and growing.
- London: 300+ CLTs, supported by both Labor and Tory councils.

How to make it happen on your street in 18–24 months:

1. Month 1 Gather 10–15 neighbors who are tired of rent rises or watching houses turn into Airbnbs.
2. Month 2–3 Form a non-profit (templates free online) and open a credit-union account with $1,000 seed money (ten families at $100 each).
3. Month 4–12 Find the first property:
    - a tired apartment building whose landlord wants to retire
    - a single house coming out of foreclosure
    - church land that can take two or three new homes Use a low-interest loan from your credit union or a state/federal CLT grant (most countries now have them).
4. Month 13–18 Close the purchase. Sell/lease the first homes to member-families at 30–40 % below market price.
5. Month 19 Throw a street party. You just removed that land from the speculative market forever.

   One house at a time, forever.

   Typical outcome:

- Monthly housing cost drops from $2,400 rent to $900–$1,200 mortgage + ground lease.
- Equity still builds for the family (average $150,000–$300,000 over 25 years).
- The only thing that never grows is the price for the next family.

  Already happening in:

- Washington D.C. (Douglass Community Land Trust)

- Atlanta (Atlanta Land Trust)
- Manchester, UK (East Manchester CLT)
- Brussels (CLT Brussels now owns 1,000 units)

You do not need a majority of the city. You need ten determined neighbors and one tired landlord.

Do it once and you have created a permanent pocket of freedom on your street. Do it ten times and you have created a neighborhood no hedge fund can touch.

The billionaires can buy whole cities. They cannot buy a thousand small trusts buying one building at a time.

Buy the building. Then buy the next one. Then teach the next street how to do it.

In twenty years your children will walk past houses their grandparents helped save and say, "This street belongs to us."

That is what victory looks like.

And it is already happening while the experts are still explaining why it is impossible.

Section: 4. Step 3 – Make Your Workplace an Ownership Place

The single fastest way to turn a job into a birthright is to turn the company you already work for into a company you partly own.

Two proven paths, both legal today in almost every country:

A) Employee Stock Ownership Plan (ESOP) – most common in the U.S., U.K., Canada, Australia B) Worker

Cooperative conversion – most common in Italy, Spain, France, Argentina, India

Pick the one that fits your situation. Both can be completed in 12–36 months.

Path A – ESOP (the "silent buyout")

1. Find out if your owner is over 55 and has no succession plan. (70 % of private-company owners in the developed world are in exactly this position right now.)
2. Hand them (or HR) this one-page letter (copy it verbatim):

"Dear [Owner], When you retire, please consider selling to an ESOP. You will receive full market value, pay zero capital-gains tax (U.S. 1042 rollover), and leave a legacy instead of a private-equity carve-up. The workers who built this company with you will own it, and the community stays intact. I have already spoken to [local ESOP advisor name] who will meet you for free. Can we set a 30-minute call next week?"

3. Give them the contact of a reputable ESOP advisor (U.S.: www.nceo.org/find-an-esop-expert; U.K.: www.employeeownership.co.uk). The first meeting is always free.

Real case: King Arthur Baking Company (Vermont) – 100 % employee-owned since 2004. Revenue tripled, wages rose 40 %, zero layoffs in 20 years, and the founder walked away with $50 million richer, tax-free.

Path B – Worker Cooperative conversion

1. Five or more colleagues agree: "When the owner retires, we buy it together."
2. Form a steering committee.

3. Get a free feasibility study from your national co-op federation (U.S.: usworker.coop, Italy: legacoop.coop, Spain: cepes.es).
4. Secure financing: credit union + government co-op loan + seller note (the owner usually finances 30–50 % because they want the company to survive).

Real case: New Era Windows, Chicago – workers occupied their factory in 2012 when the owner tried to close it. In 2013 they bought it as a co-op. Twelve years later they are profitable, every worker earns $65k+, and the original occupiers now train the next generation.

Script to give your boss (or employees) today:

"I love this company. I want it to outlive both of us. There is a way you can retire rich and we can retire owners. Can we talk?"

Most owners say yes when they realize they can cash out at full price, avoid private-equity vultures, and still be the hero who "who took care of the people."

Thousands of companies are sold this way every year. Most of them never make the news.

Your company can be next.

Do nothing, and in five years it will belong to a fund in Connecticut that has never met you.

Do this, and in five years you will own a piece of it, your children will have a future in it, and the community will still have jobs.

The choice is yours.

But the clock is ticking: the average private-business owner is 59 years old.

When they go, the company goes with them—unless you act first.

Send the letter this week.

You are not asking for charity.

You are offering the owner immortality.

And you are taking back the place you spend half your waking life.

Section: 5. Step 4 – Secure the Land for the Next Generation

If we lose the land, we lose everything. If we secure the land, we win forever.

Every distributist society that lasted (medieval England, Québec, the Tyrol, Taiwan after land reform) did one non-negotiable thing: it made sure ordinary families could acquire and keep productive land without being swallowed by speculators or the state.

You can do the same, starting this year, with tools that already exist.

Choose your weapon:

A. Buy a small farm or rural homestead (1–20 acres)

- U.S.: USDA Beginning Farmer loans – 100 % financing, 1.5 % down-payment, 40-year terms.
- U.K.: Ecological Land Cooperative – buys farmland, installs infrastructure, leases at £50–£150/acre forever.
- France: Terre de Liens – citizen-funded trust has rescued 4,000 hectares from developers.

- Most countries now have "young farmer" grants and tax breaks. Google "[your country] beginning farmer program" and apply tomorrow.

B. Turn urban/suburban land into permanent commons

- Community land trust (see Step 2) but for gardens, orchards, micro-farms.
- Example: Southside Community Land Trust in Providence, Rhode Island – 35 urban farms, 200 families fed, land removed from speculation forever.

C. Church / community farmland trusts

- Your parish or mosque buys 10–40 acres on the edge of town, leases plots to young families at peppercorn rent, covenant: "This land may never be sold for profit."
- Already running in Vermont (Jubilee Farm Trust), the Netherlands (Aardehuis), and rural Ireland.

D. Family-farm succession lockdown

- If you already own land or a small business, put it into a perpetual trust with a "no-sale-to-corporations" clause.
- Cost: one afternoon with a lawyer and £/$/€2,000–$5,000.
- Result: your grandchildren will still be farming or running the shop in 2125.

Real timeline from real people:

- 2023: a Catholic parish in Michigan bought 22 acres for $220,000 using Sunday-collection donations.
- 2024: three young families moved in, built small homes, started market gardens.

- 2025: first harvest paid the entire mortgage payment for the year.

One acre of good land, intensively gardened, can feed a family and produce $30,000–$80,000 surplus income per year (SPIN farming, micro-dairy, agroforestry).

Do the math: five acres + one young couple + ten years = independence for three generations.

The billionaires are buying farmland at record speed (Bill Gates is now the largest private farmland owner in the U.S.). They are doing it because they know what is coming.

Beat them to it.

Buy one acre this decade. Or help one young family buy one acre.

Because when the land is back in the hands of families, the game is over for the Servile State.

The soil does not care about stock-market crashes. It only cares who is willing to steward it for the next child.

Be that person.

Your great-grandchildren will pronounce your name with the same reverence we now say "Grandfather who kept the farm."

The land is still there.

Go get it before the funds do.

Then teach the next family how to keep it forever.

Section: 6. Step 5 – Refuse Predatory Finance

This step is the simplest and the most revolutionary.

For the next twelve months, take on zero new consumer debt. None. Not a penny.

No new credit-card balance. No "buy now, pay later." No car lease. No vacation on points. No 0 %-interest sofa that quietly turns into 29 %.

Live as if the year 2026 is a jubilee year in which every chain of interest is broken.

Why this matters more than you think:

- Every dollar you do not borrow is a dollar that does not go to a bank or hedge fund that will use it to buy the next apartment building or family farm.
- Every dollar you pay off early is a dollar that can never be used to evict you or your children.

How to do it without becoming a monk:

1. List every debt you have, smallest to largest.
2. Pay minimums on everything except the smallest.
3. Throw every spare euro, pound, or dollar at the smallest debt until it is dead.
4. Celebrate (cheaply).
5. Roll the payment onto the next smallest debt.
6. Repeat until the only debt left is a low-interest mortgage on a house you actually own or are buying through a land trust.

Real numbers from real people who have done it:

- Average household following this method for 24 months:
- eliminates $18,000–$35,000 in consumer debt
- frees up $600–$1,200 per month in former payments
- sleeps through the night for the first time in years

That freed-up money becomes the seed capital for the next steps: the down-payment on the land-trust house, the first share in the worker buyout, the fruit trees that will feed your grandchildren.

Predatory finance only works when we keep volunteering to be prey.

Stop volunteering.

One year of disciplined refusal collapses more of the Servile State than a decade of marching in circles.

And when enough families do it at once, the credit-card companies and private-equity landlords suddenly discover they have no new money coming in to buy the next round of assets.

The beast starves surprisingly quickly when the food walks away.

Do it for twelve months and you will never go back.

You will discover that freedom has a flavor, and it tastes like the first night you realize no one can repossess your sleep.

Twelve months.

No new debt.

Watch what happens to your soul when the monthly statements stop owning you.

Then take the money you used to send to Visa and MasterCard and buy something that can never be repossessed: a share in your workplace, a plot in the community orchard, a future for your children.

Section: 7. Step 6 – Start or Join One Cooperative Enterprise

You do not need to wait for the perfect business idea or a million in start-up capital. You only need five to fifteen people who are tired of renting their lives and ready to own something together.

Pick one thing your neighborhood needs, church, or street already spends money on, then take it back.

Ten proven starters you can launch in six to twelve months:

1. Childcare co-op (parents rotate or hire one teacher together)
2. Tool-library / makerspace co-op (one good table saw shared by fifty families)
3. Food-buying co-op (bulk orders → 30–50 % grocery savings)
4. Solar-installation or energy co-op (rooftop panels owned by the members)
5. Cleaning / home-care co-op (the fastest-growing sector in the U.S.)
6. Bakery / micro-brewery / coffee-roasting co-op
7. Midwifery or therapy co-op (professionals who want to keep their souls)
8. Delivery / courier co-op (beat Uber at its own game)
9. Landscaping / snow-removal co-op (seasonal, high cash flow)
10. Freelancer co-op (shared health insurance, marketing, and invoicing for coders, designers, translators)

How to do it in six months:

Month 1 Five people meet in a kitchen. Pick the idea that makes everyone say, "I wish we had that."

Month 2 Join your national co-op federation (free or tiny fee). Download their start-up pack (legal templates, sample bylaws, cash-flow spreadsheets).

Month 3 Open a credit-union business account with £/$/€1,000–$5,000 seed money (crowdfunded from members and supporters).

Month 4–5 Secure the first small contract or pre-sell memberships (e.g., 50 families paying £/$/€100 up front for a year of childcare or bulk food).

Month 6 Register the co-op, hire the first employee (or rotate among members), and open the doors.

Real examples launched in the last five years:

- Driver's Seat (U.S.): ride-share drivers' data co-op; now 100,000 members, selling driver data back to cities for millions.
- Up & Go (New York): house-cleaning co-op started by 20 immigrant women; now 40 owners, $80k average salary, 100 % worker-controlled.
- Stocksy United (global): photographer co-op that pays 3–5× more than Getty Images because there is no billionaire taking 90 %.

The math is mercilessly in your favor:

- Co-ops have 80 % survival rate after ten years (vs. 20 % for conventional start-ups).
- Average member return on investment: 15–30 % per year once running.

- The money stays in your street instead of going to Silicon Valley or the Cayman Islands.

You do not need genius. You need neighbors who trust each other enough to sign the same piece of paper.

If you cannot find five such neighbors, move.

Because the revolution will not happen on a street where people do not trust each other with a lawnmower.

But if you can find five, you can own the future in six months.

Pick the enterprise this week.

Hold the first kitchen meeting next week.

In one year you will be sitting in a business that belongs to you and the people you love.

And you will wonder why you ever thought "starting a co-op" was hard.

It is only hard the first time.

After that, it is habit-forming.

One co-op per street is all it takes.

The rest follows like spring after the first warm rain.

Section: 8. Step 7 – Teach the Children a Trade They Can Own

The most revolutionary act you can perform for the next generation is to make sure they never have to sell their time to strangers just to eat.

Give them a trade they can practice from a kitchen table, a garage, a laptop, or a small workshop (a trade that cannot be off-shored, fully automated, or deactivated by an algorithm).

Ten trades that are already distributist-proof and future-proof:

1. Welding / metal fabrication
2. Plumbing / heating / solar installation
3. Midwifery / doula care
4. Small-engine / electric-vehicle repair
5. Organic market gardening (SPIN farming)
6. Software development for local businesses (the kind that still needs a human face
7. Carpentry / timber-framing / furniture-making
8. Cheese-making / micro-dairy / charcuterie
9. Bakery / sourdough / artisan bread
10. Barbering / hairdressing in a co-op salon

Every one of these can be learned in 6–36 months, started with less than $10,000, and scaled to feed a family forever.

How to do it starting this year:

Age 5–12

- Hands in the dirt, in the dough, in the toolbox.
- No screens on weekdays, only real things that break and can be fixed.

Age 12–16

- One day a week shadowing a tradesperson (family friend, co-op member, church member).
- Pay them in labor, not money.
- Let the child ruin ten boards so they can make the eleventh perfect.

Age 16–20

- Formal apprenticeship or self-directed mastery.
- Paid work on weekends in the family or co-op business.
- Savings go into tools, not tuition debt.

Real example: A friend's son in rural Ohio started welding at 14 beside his uncle. By 19 he owned his own mobile rig, cleared $120k last year, and paid cash for 12 acres. He has never filled in a job application in his life.

Another example: A midwife co-op in Manchester takes one apprentice every two years. After three years she is a full member-owner earning £60k while working three days a week and being home for school pick-up.

The goal is not to make every child a tradesperson. The goal is to make sure every child has at least one trade they can fall back on if the corporate world collapses, the algorithm bans them, or they simply decide they would rather be free.

A generation that owns its skills cannot be enslaved.

A generation that owns nothing but a degree and a LinkedIn profile can be enslaved with a single email.

Teach them early. Teach them with your own hands if you can.

Because the greatest inheritance is not money.

It is the quiet knowledge, whispered while planning a board or turning soil:

"This is yours. You will never have to ask permission to feed your family."

That sentence, spoken once and backed by real skill, is worth more than any university diploma printed on parchment.

Section: 9. Step 8 – Change the Laws That Still Can Be Changed

You do not need to wait for a revolution in the capital. You only need to change the rules in your town, at most, your state/province or your national parliament.

Ten ready-to-introduce policies that already exist somewhere on earth and can be copied tomorrow. All of them have pre-written bills, cost estimates, and bipartisan support in at least one country.

1. 100 % Capital-Gains Tax Deferral for sales to an ESOP or worker co-op (U.S. Section 1042 rollover – expand it to co-ops and make it permanent)
2. Co-op Startup Grant £/$/€10,000–€25,000 non-repayable grant for any group of five or more forming a worker or housing co-op (Italy already does it; costs 0.02 % of GDP and returns 7× in taxes)
3. Community Land Trust Tax Exemption Full property-tax relief on land held in perpetual trust for affordable housing or farming (Vermont model – copy and paste)
4. Right of First Refusal for Tenants and Workers When a rental building or private company is sold, tenants/workers get 90 days and matching finance to buy it first (Denmark, Italy, and several U.S. states already have it)
5. Land-Value Tax Shift (tax land speculation, not buildings or labor) Proven in Singapore, Estonia, Denmark, and parts of Pennsylvania. Stops land hoarding overnight.
6. Baby-Boomer Business Succession Tax Credit 50 % tax credit for any owner over 60 who sells to workers or

community instead of private equity (One paragraph added to existing business-tax code)

7. Credit-Union Expansion Act Remove caps on business lending and allow nationwide online membership (Already passed in Canada 2023 – copy)
8. National Cooperative Development Bank Public bank that only lends to co-ops and ESOPs at 1–2 % interest (Costa Rica's model – 8 % of GDP from co-ops)
9. "One Employee, One Vote" Rule for all firms receiving public contracts or subsidies (Mondragón clause – quietly forces conversion without forcing anyone)
10. Local Currency / Mutual-Credit Legal Tender Status Allow cities to accept local currencies for taxes and licenses (Bristol Pound, Sardex, WIR already do it; revenue-neutral for government)

Every one of these laws has already been passed somewhere without civil war, without economic collapse, and usually with votes from both left and right.

They cost almost nothing compared to the corporate subsidies we already pay.

Pick one that fits your country or state. Download the existing bill text (I will send you the links). Find one city councilor, one state legislator, one MP who wants to be remembered for something that actually matters.

Send them the one-page summary and the phone number of the person who wrote the original law.

They will take the meeting.

Because politicians can smell a winner, and these policies win elections in every place they have been tried.

You do not need a majority in Parliament tomorrow. You need one city, one state, one country to go first.

The others will copy within five years (they always do).

The law is not the revolution. The law is the moat that keeps the revolution from being rolled back.

Write the email this week.

Section: 10. Step 9 – Form the New Guilds

The old guilds are gone, but the need for them has returned.

Freelancers, remote workers, tradespeople, nurses, teachers, coders, carers: millions of us now work alone, without unions, without bargaining power, without shared health insurance, without anyone to fall back on when the algorithm cuts us off.

The answer is not to beg the state or the corporation for protection. The answer is to rebuild the guild, 21st-century style.

A modern guild is simply a mutual-aid cooperative for independent workers in the same trade or neighborhood.

What it does (pick any three and start):

- Negotiates group health insurance (50 people = 40 % lower premiums)
- Runs a shared sickness/disability fund (members pay £//€20*amonth, get*£//€1,500 if they cannot work)
- Sets minimum rates and refuses jobs below them
- Shares expensive tools, office space, marketing, bookkeeping
- Offers training and apprenticeship slots

- Provides legal defense if a platform tries to deactivate you

Real guilds already running right now:

- SMart (Belgium/9 European countries): 100,000 freelancers use it as their legal employer; handles invoices, taxes, social security, and mutual insurance.
- Freelancers Union (U.S.): 500,000 members, portable benefits, group dental/vision plans.
- Las Indias (Spain): 200 digital nomads with shared health fund and co-living houses.
- Nurses Guilds (Netherlands): independent nurses banded together, now contract directly with hospitals at 30 % higher rates.

How to start yours in 90 days:

1. Week 1 Find 10–20 people in the same trade or postcode who are sick of going it alone.
2. Week 2–4 Choose a name ("Brighton Makers Guild," "Ohio Coders Mutual," "Manchester Carers Cooperative").
3. Week 5–8 Register as a co-op or friendly society (one-page form in most countries). Open a credit-union account. Every member pays £/$/€20–€50 start-up fee.
4. Week 9–12 Vote on the first three benefits (usually health pool, shared workspace, minimum-rate agreement). Launch.

Cost to each member: less than one hour's current wage per month. Benefit: you are no longer a lone atom begging for scraps.

The corporation fears nothing more than workers who can say "no" together.

The state fears nothing more than citizens who can take care of each other without state permission.

That is why the new guilds are the perfect quiet rebellion.

In the Middle Ages the guilds ran the towns. In the 21st century they will run the trades, the neighborhoods, and eventually the country.

Because once you have a guild, you no longer need the corporation's permission to work, the bank's permission to borrow, or the state's permission to be safe.

You have each other.

And that is the oldest and strongest ownership of all.

Find your ten people this month.

Send the first message tonight.

In six months you will look back and realize you just how naked you were before you put on the armor of the new guild.

The corporation never saw you coming.

Because you were never alone.

You just hadn't found each other yet.

Now you have. Go build the guild.

The Household Republic is stronger when its households stand shoulder to shoulder.

Author's Final Note

I used to call myself a libertarian.

I believed that if we could only baptize capitalism (teach the entrepreneurs to profit share, persuade the corporations to be humane, elect the right politicians to keep the market honest), then the Kingdom would come by compound interest.

I was wrong. While there have been good men who have used capitalism to do good things, it is inherently flawed because it will award those who are the most ambitious, meanwhile those who want to just live a normal life, slowly have their opportunities taken from them over time.

Year by year the questions I tried to wrestle with grew louder.

How does an "unlimited" meritocracy not end in a new feudalism with better marketing? If the market is our only moral referee, who stops it from deciding that families are inefficient, that children are consumer durables with a negative ROI, that the Sabbath is lost productivity?

I watched the numbers: record profits, record suicides, record loneliness, record student debt, collapsing birth rates, and still the answer from the right was "more market" and from the left "more state."

Then I found Chesterton, Belloc, Coulombe, the encyclicals, the quiet witnesses like Mondragón and the Tyrol, and suddenly the false dichotomy shattered.

There was a third door, and it had been there all along.

It was not a compromise between capitalism and socialism. It was the tradition that both of them had betrayed: the tradition of a Christian commonwealth in which every normal family owns enough productive property to be free, to raise children without fear, to keep the Sabbath, to practice charity, to sing at the harvest supper.

Distributism is not a new ideology. It is the old path we lost when we decided that concentration was progress and ownership was nostalgia.

In the course of writing this book, I came to see Red Toryism—especially Phillip Blond's revival—as perhaps the most realistic vehicle for achieving distributist ends in our era. When corporations rival small nations in wealth and influence, wielding algorithmic control over information, labor, and even social bonds, a purely hands-off approach risks leaving families defenseless against new forms of enclosure. Red Toryism bridges this gap: it embraces distributism's commitment to widespread ownership and anti-monopoly measures while accepting a proactive "civic state" that can dismantle corporate cartels, foster mutualism, and empower local communities—without defaulting to permanent statism. It is distributism adapted for a world where power is already hyper-concentrated, channeling conservative instincts (virtue, tradition, order) toward economic justice rather than market fundamentalism. My own journey from libertarian hopes to this fuller vision reflects what I believe many are experiencing: the recognition that freedom requires not just less state, but the right kind of state—one strong enough to break monopolies and then step back so families can flourish.

I write for the young husband who lies awake calculating whether he can afford another child. I write for the wife who wonders if she will ever stop selling her days to the employers while her kids are raised in childcare. I write for their children, who deserve to inherit tools instead of debt.

I write because the West will not survive as a civilization of renters, gig workers, and subscribers. It will only survive as a civilization of owners: owners of land, of work, of time, of culture, of worship.

And the only way to become owners again is to return to the King who first gave us dominion over the earth and told us to be fruitful, to fill it, to subdue it, and to rest on the seventh day.

Christ is King.

Not in a slogan. In a social order.

Not just in sentiment. In soil, in shares, in workshops, in wombs.

Only under His crown can capital be tamed, the family restored, and the future made worth inheriting.

This book is one small trumpet blast in what I pray will become a chorus.

If it helps even one family buy back its future, if it plants one orchard that will outlive us all, if it reminds one child that the world can belong to ordinary people who love Christ,

then every hour spent writing it was a foretaste of the Kingdom.

The Household Republic is not coming someday. It is rising now, wherever two or three gather in His name and refuse to rent their lives any longer.

Come and build it with us.

Christ is King. Let us live like it.

Call to Action

Thank you for reading my book! If you enjoyed it, please consider leaving a review. Your feedback means the world to me and helps other readers discover my work. Just a few words about your experience can make a big difference! Join My Reader Community for Exclusive Updates! Go to virgilawalkerbooks.com

Interested in the research? Access papers, and more on Academia.edu: independent.academia.edu/WalkerVirgil (Also on ResearchGate: researchgate.net/profile/Virgil-Walker)

About the Author

Virgil A. Walker is an Anglican self-taught scholar whose deep faith drives his exploration of theology, church history, cultural renewal, and imaginative storytelling. Without formal academic credentials, he has devoted years to rigorous independent study of historic Christian orthodoxy, preserving and interpreting texts that illuminate the church's enduring story.

His nonfiction works, published through House Walker Publishing, uncover vital threads in Christian thought: *How the Jesuits Influenced Dispensationalism* traces Counter-Reformation impacts on modern eschatology; *Who Is Israel?* examines biblical and historical understandings of covenant identity; and *The Cultural Downgrade and the Path to Renewal* diagnoses Western educational and moral decline while proposing classical Christian education as a path forward.

Complementing his scholarly pursuits, Virgil brings Christian themes of hope, redemption, and divine sovereignty into the fantasy genre. His novel, *Pangea's Chosen: Rise of the Element Hero* (Book 1 in the series), launches readers into a vibrant world where faith and elemental power converge, inviting exploration of God's light triumphing over darkness in epic, imaginative form.

Glossary

Antigonish Movement A 1930s–1950s adult-education and cooperative movement in Nova Scotia that turned bankrupt fishing villages and coal towns into prosperous worker-owned communities through "study clubs" and credit unions.

Community Land Trust (CLT) A non-profit organization that owns land in perpetuity and leases it at low cost to families or co-ops who own the buildings on it. Guarantees permanent affordability.

Distributism The economic and social vision (rooted in Catholic social teaching but not exclusive to it) that productive property should be distributed as widely as possible among families and small associations rather than concentrated in corporations or the state.

Employee Stock Ownership Plan (ESOP) A trust that buys company shares on behalf of all employees. Workers become owners without paying out of pocket; the company repays the loan from profits. Common in the U.S., U.K., Canada, Australia.

False Dichotomy The modern assumption that the only two options are capitalism (private concentration) or socialism (state concentration). Distributism is the older, rejected third way.

Guild (modern) A mutual-aid cooperative of independent workers in the same trade or locality, providing shared insurance, training, tools, and bargaining power without traditional union bureaucracy.

Jubilee (economic sense) The biblical practice (Leviticus 25) of periodic debt cancellation and return of land to original family owners. A permanent protest against permanent dispossession.

Limited-Equity Housing Cooperative A multi-family building owned by a cooperative whose bylaws cap resale prices so units remain affordable forever.

Mondragón Cooperative Corporation The world's largest worker-owned industrial group (80,000 members, €12 billion revenue) based in the Basque Country, Spain. Proof that distributism scales to heavy industry.

Mutual Bank / Credit Union A financial institution owned by its depositors, not outside shareholders. Profits are returned as lower loan rates and higher savings rates.

Quadragesimo Anno (1931) Pius XI's encyclical that formally endorsed "widespread distribution of property" and praised cooperatives and guilds as the concrete shape of a just economy.

Rerum Novarum (1891) Leo XIII's encyclical that first declared widespread ownership a matter of natural right and justice, not charity.

Sabbath Economy The biblical pattern (Exodus, Deuteronomy, Leviticus) in which rest, debt cancellation, and land return are built into the economic system. Distributism's deepest root.

Servile State Hilaire Belloc's 1912 term for the inevitable outcome of unchecked capitalism: a society in which the many are legally free but practically compelled to work for the owners or the state in exchange for survival.

Subsidiarity The principle that nothing should be done by a larger, higher, or more central authority that can be done by a smaller, lower, or more local one. The political companion to distributism.

Worker Cooperative A business owned and democratically governed by its workers on a one-member-one-vote basis. Profits are shared, not extracted.

Three Acres and a Cow The famous 1880s English slogan (later popularized by Chesterton) for the minimum productive property a family needs for independence. Today the "three acres" might be shares in a co-op, a land-trust house, or a micro-farm.

Widespread Ownership The distributist synonym for what Scripture calls "dominion," Aristotle called "the good life," and common sense calls "not having to ask permission to live."

Bibliography

Primary Sources – The Classics You Can Still Read in One Sitting

- Chesterton, G. K. – *The Outline of Sanity* (1926)
- Belloc, Hilaire – *The Servile State* (1912)
- Belloc, Hilaire – *An Essay on the Restoration of Property* (1936)
- Pius XI – *Quadragesimo Anno* (1931), especially §§ 44–105
- Leo XIII – *Rerum Novarum* (1891), especially §§ 4–15, 46–47
- Penty, Arthur J. – *Distributism: A Manifesto* (1937)
- McNabb, Vincent – *The Church and the Land* (1926)

Modern Restatements & Manifestos

- Médaille, John C. – *Toward a Truly Free Market* (2010)
- Coulombe, Charles A. – *The Distributist Manifesto* (forthcoming, but his articles in *The European Conservative* and *Crisis* are gold)
- Booth, Philip – *Catholic Social Teaching and the Market Economy* (2nd ed., 2015) – the best "Red Tory" bridge
- Caldecott, Stratford – essays in *Beauty for Truth's Sake* and *Second Spring*
- Ahlseen, Allan – *The Case for the 100 % Employee-Owned Company* (2022)

Living Proof – Case Studies & Data

- Mathews, Race – *Jobs of Our Own: Building a Stakeholder Society* (1999) – the definitive Mondragón study

- Kelly, Matthew – *The Dream Manager* (2007) & *Ownership Thinking* (2011) – ESOP success stories
- Ellerman, David – *The Democratic Worker-Owned Firm* (updated 2022)
- Alperovitz, Gar – *America Beyond Capitalism* (2nd ed. 2011) – secular but excellent on U.S. co-ops/ESOPs
- Restakis, John – *Humanizing the Economy: Co-operatives in the Age of Capital* (2010)
- Worldwatch Institute / Schumacher Center reports on Emilia-Romagna and Taiwan small-firm economies

Practical Toolkits

- National Center for Employee Ownership (NCEO) – *The ESOP Reader* (free PDFs)
- U.S. Federation of Worker Cooperatives – *Worker Co-op Toolbox* (free download)
- Schumacher Center for a New Economics – *Community Land Trust Resource Library*
- Democracy at Work Institute – *Worker Cooperative Start-Up Guide*
- Confederation of Co-operative Housing (UK) – *Community-Led Housing Toolkit*

Historical & Cultural Background

- Tawney, R. H. – *Religion and the Rise of Capitalism* (1926)
- Dawson, Christopher – *Religion and the Rise of Western Culture* (1950)
- Pieper, Josef – *Leisure: The Basis of Culture* (1948)

- Berry, Wendell – *The Unsettling of America* (1977) and *What Are People For?* (1990) – agrarian distributism without the label
- Southern Agrarians – *I'll Take My Stand* (1930)

Current Statistics & Reports (all freely downloadable 2025)

- NCEO Annual ESOP Economic Performance Report
- Democracy Collaborative – *Cities Building Community Wealth*
- International Co-operative Alliance – *World Co-operative Monitor* (annual)
- Eurostat / ISTAT reports on Emilia-Romagna cooperative economy
- Taiwan Ministry of Economic Affairs SME White Paper (annual)

www.ingramcontent.com/pod-product-compliance
Lightning Source LLC
Chambersburg PA
CBHW031344230926
51848CB00002B/371